Unreal Engine Virtual Reality Quick Start Guide

Design and Develop immersive virtual reality experiences with Unreal Engine 4

Jessica Plowman

BIRMINGHAM - MUMBAI

Unreal Engine Virtual Reality Quick Start Guide

Commissioning Editor: Kunal Chaudhari
Acquisition Editor: Siddharth Mandal
Content Development Editor: Smit Carvalho
Technical Editor: Leena Patil
Copy Editor: Safis Editing
Project Coordinator: Pragati Shukla
Proofreader: Safis Editing
Indexer: Pratik Shirodkar
Graphics: Alishon Mendonsa
Production Coordinator: Saili Kale

First published: February 2019

Production reference:1260219

Published by Packt Publishing Ltd.
Livery Place
35 Livery Street
Birmingham
B3 2PB, UK.

ISBN 978-1-78961-740-5

www.packtpub.com

To my wife, Jennifer, and our family for loving and supporting me through this process. I could not do this without you. To my students, past and present – I do this for you, and everyone like you, who wants to live their dream.

– Jessica Plowman

`mapt.io`

Mapt is an online digital library that gives you full access to over 5,000 books and videos, as well as industry leading tools to help you plan your personal development and advance your career. For more information, please visit our website.

Why subscribe?

- Spend less time learning and more time coding with practical eBooks and Videos from over 4,000 industry professionals

- Improve your learning with Skill Plans built especially for you

- Get a free eBook or video every month

- Mapt is fully searchable

- Copy and paste, print, and bookmark content

Packt.com

Did you know that Packt offers eBook versions of every book published, with PDF and ePub files available? You can upgrade to the eBook version at `www.packt.com` and as a print book customer, you are entitled to a discount on the eBook copy. Get in touch with us at `customercare@packtpub.com` for more details.

At `www.packt.com`, you can also read a collection of free technical articles, sign up for a range of free newsletters, and receive exclusive discounts and offers on Packt books and eBooks.

Contributors

About the author

Jessica Plowman is a game designer and educator who currently resides in the United States. At an early age, she discovered her love for video games and the joy they bring to others. She began teaching students about game development in 2005 and enjoys supporting the dreams of the next generation of developers. She has worked with Unreal technology for over 10 years, and currently teaches students game technology and game design in Sarasota, Florida. When not teaching, she consults on different topics related to Unreal technology and continues to further her education by researching best practices related to both teaching and game development.

No one completes projects like this alone and I am no exception. I would like to thank my beautiful and patient wife, Jennifer, for all her care and support during the writing and development process. Without her, my life would be empty. As always, I also want to thank the UE4 community and the folks at Tribe XR. We all stand on the shoulders of those who came before us, so thank you.

About the reviewer

Deepak Jadhav is a game developer based in Pune, India. Deepak received his BSc in computer technology and MSc in game programming and project management. Currently, he is working as a game developer in a leading game development company in India. He has been involved in developing games on multiple platforms, including PC, macOS, and mobile. With years of experience in game development, he has a strong background in C# and C++, as well as the skills he has built up on platforms including Unity, the Unreal Engine, and augmented and virtual reality.

I would like to thank the author and the Packt Publishing team for giving me the opportunity to review this book.

Packt is searching for authors like you

If you're interested in becoming an author for Packt, please visit `authors.packtpub.com` and apply today. We have worked with thousands of developers and tech professionals, just like you, to help them share their insight with the global tech community. You can make a general application, apply for a specific hot topic that we are recruiting an author for, or submit your own idea.

Table of Contents

Preface

For many of us developers, **Virtual Reality** (**VR**) represents a relatively untapped market for unique games that take advantage of an amazing new technology. VR has the ability to drop our players directly into our digital worlds and provide them with an experience they cannot get anywhere else. However, the skills that are needed to adopt this new technology and create these worlds are not yet widespread and easy to come by. Our goal is to change this and help spread the word about the power of VR.

Epic Games has been a long-time supporter of VR. Over the last several versions, Unreal Engine 4 has expanded its support for VR and continues to optimize its software to allow more developers to do amazing things. On the hardware side of things, both the number of manufacturers and the capabilities of the VR headsets on the market continue to increase. Many developers are making apps for the Oculus Rift and HTC Vive, though there are several other options to choose from, including PlayStation VR, Samsung Gear VR, and Windows Mixed Reality Headsets.

Whichever you choose, this book can help you on your journey of working with VR. Over the course of the book, we will look at how to design for VR. We will program flexible interaction systems for this unique environment, create user interface elements, and discuss the specific game art needs of the medium. Finally, we will wrap up with a game prototype and prepare it for distribution.

Who this book is for

This book is written for the intermediate to advanced user of Unreal Engine 4 with an interest in working with VR technology. These users are familiar with the game engine, but have not yet explored how to create games and applications in VR.

What this book covers

Chapter 1, *Introducing VR Technology in Unreal Engine 4*, will give you a solid introduction to VR technology in Unreal Engine 4 and to the types of virtual reality hardware that are available on the market today. We discuss the current limitations of the hardware and introduce you to our sample project, *Server 17*.

Chapter 2, *Locomotion, Design, and Starting Our Project*, guides you through the different types of movement systems currently in use in modern VR games, and discusses the pros and cons of each. Using human-centered design methods, you will design a locomotion system for first-time players and go through the process to set up our sample game in Unreal Engine 4.

Chapter 3, *Exploring Riveting Gameplay in Virtual Reality*, has you delving into different types of gameplay used in popular virtual reality titles such as *Gorn, Tribe XR*, and others. You are then guided through designing gameplay for our sample game, and building movement and interaction systems from scratch using Unreal Engine 4's powerful blueprint system.

Chapter 4, *User Interface and User Experience inside VR*, teaches the basics of user experience design and how these techniques are applied to virtual reality. The book explores 2D and 3D interface elements, and guides you through creating both.

Chapter 5, *Creating Optimized Game Art for VR in UE4*, discusses the limitations that VR software and hardware place on creating game art. You will explore the issues surrounding the creation of 3D models, textures/materials, lighting, and visual effects, as well as some best practices for dealing with those limitations.

Chapter 6, *Finalizing Our VR Game and Next Steps*, completes the journey of game creation by discussing the importance of game testing, outlines some techniques to gather testing data, and discusses how to improve your design based on feedback. You are taken through the steps for finalizing the sample game for distribution, and we'll look at where to go next with the game prototype that you have developed.

To get the most out of this book

- An intermediate knowledge of the Unreal game engine is required for this book
- An installation of Unreal Engine 4.20.x is required
- A virtual reality headset and the computer hardware capable of running it are required

Download the example code files

You can download the example code files for this book from your account at www.packt.com. If you purchased this book elsewhere, you can visit www.packt.com/support and register to have the files emailed directly to you.

You can download the code files by following these steps:

1. Log in or register at `www.packt.com`.
2. Select the **SUPPORT** tab.
3. Click on **Code Downloads & Errata**.
4. Enter the name of the book in the **Search** box and follow the onscreen instructions.

Once the file is downloaded, please make sure that you unzip or extract the folder using the latest version of:

- WinRAR/7-Zip for Windows
- Zipeg/iZip/UnRarX for Mac
- 7-Zip/PeaZip for Linux

The code bundle for the book is also hosted on GitHub at `https://github.com/PacktPublishing/Unreal-Engine-Virtual-Reality-Quick-Start-Guide`. In case there's an update to the code, it will be updated on the existing GitHub repository.

We also have other code bundles from our rich catalog of books and videos available at `https://github.com/PacktPublishing/`. Check them out!

Download the color images

We also provide a PDF file that has color images of the screenshots/diagrams used in this book. You can download it here: `https://www.packtpub.com/sites/default/files/downloads/9781789617405_ColorImages.pdf`.

Conventions used

There are a number of text conventions used throughout this book.

Bold: Indicates a new term, an important word, or words that you see onscreen. For example, words in menus or dialog boxes appear in the text like this. Here is an example: "Smack that **Create Project** button and let's continue! Now take a look at the interface."

 Warnings or important notes appear like this.

Tips and tricks appear like this.

Get in touch

Feedback from our readers is always welcome.

General feedback: If you have questions about any aspect of this book, mention the book title in the subject of your message and email us at customercare@packtpub.com.

Errata: Although we have taken every care to ensure the accuracy of our content, mistakes do happen. If you have found a mistake in this book, we would be grateful if you would report this to us. Please visit www.packt.com/submit-errata, selecting your book, clicking on the Errata Submission Form link, and entering the details.

Piracy: If you come across any illegal copies of our works in any form on the Internet, we would be grateful if you would provide us with the location address or website name. Please contact us at copyright@packt.com with a link to the material.

If you are interested in becoming an author: If there is a topic that you have expertise in and you are interested in either writing or contributing to a book, please visit authors.packtpub.com.

Reviews

Please leave a review. Once you have read and used this book, why not leave a review on the site that you purchased it from? Potential readers can then see and use your unbiased opinion to make purchase decisions, we at Packt can understand what you think about our products, and our authors can see your feedback on their book. Thank you!

For more information about Packt, please visit packt.com.

Introducing VR Technology in Unreal Engine 4

1

Virtual Reality (VR). These words call to mind images of movies from the 1980s and 1990s, such as characters such as The Lawnmower Man, people strapped into equipment that covers their entire bodies, and computers that take up entire rooms, as well as digital vistas that stretch forever and basic geometric shapes that were meant to simulate the real world. The term VR came about in the 1980s to refer to the systems of gloves and headgear that are used to interact with these computer-generated worlds. Since then, advances in electronics and digital displays have allowed for the creation of smaller, more powerful devices. In 2010, Palmer Lucky's discovery that mobile phone display technology had reached a high enough resolution to be used in VR led to the creation of the first Oculus Rift headset. This event would kick-off the technology arms race that has since given us the Oculus Rift, the Samsung Gear VR, the HTC Vive, and the new Windows Mixed Reality headsets. With the prices coming down every year, VR has found its way into the hands of 171 million users around the world.

For many of you, this book represents the first steps down the path to creating your very own VR title. You may have recently grown interested in getting started with the technology, or you might already have a complete design, and you are ready to begin developing. In either case, this book will lead you through the process of choosing your target hardware and audience, the unique design, locomotion, and gameplay concepts specific to VR, creating art for your virtual world, and finally the process of testing and prepping your game for distribution. Through the creation of our sample game, *Server 17*, we will discuss some of the problems VR developers face, such as optimization and how to help players deal with VR sickness.

This book assumes that readers have a working knowledge of Unreal Engine 4 and access to VR equipment. If you are just starting out with Unreal Engine 4, I recommend checking out my other title, *3D Game Design with Unreal Engine 4 and Blender*, or any of the other great game development titles from Packt Publishing before coming back to this one.

In this chapter, we will cover the following topics:

- Why use Unreal Engine 4 for VR?
- What types of VR technology are available to developers?
- Pros and cons of popular VR headsets
- Limitations of VR
- Introducing our sample project—*Server 17*

Why use Unreal Engine 4 for VR?

VR represents the next great frontier for game developers. Just like mobile technology allowed for developers to reach new markets and move video games into the mainstream, VR gaming will also be able to tap into new markets and appeal to new fans who are looking for a more active style of gaming. To accommodate this, game engine developers have been quickly working to add new features and refine existing ones to entice developers to choose their platform for their next big title:

Robo Recall was one of the first standout tiles that was built for VR using Unreal Engine 4. Image courtesy of Epic Games

Beginning in 2014, Epic Games began laying the groundwork for full VR support within Unreal. This led to the development of their first VR title, *Robo Recall*. In this game, players were able to shoot and smash their way through a city overrun by murderous machines. The game utilized a teleportation system for locomotion and some pretty solid controls for its gun-based gameplay. The game began development in 2016 and was released for Oculus Rift in 2017. It took full advantage of the most recent build of Unreal at the time to show off the latest rendering techniques and optimizations for VR.

Since then, Epic Games has continued to update and develop Unreal Engine 4 to provide game developers with the best tools available for their projects. Unreal Engine versions 4.17, 4.18, and 4.19 included many optimizations and performance updates geared specifically toward VR headsets and VR developers, with the goal of being able to improve performance and framerates, two of the most crucial elements to monitor in VR game development.

Beyond a commitment to bringing developers the best tools for their VR games, Epic Games provides developers with many other reasons to choose Unreal Engine for their games:

- Unreal Engine is free to begin using, with only a 5% royalty after the first $3,000 per game per quarter. These terms allow smaller teams of developers to dive right into projects without worrying about how to pay for their tools.
- Unreal provides support for most VR hardware, including the Samsung Gear VR, the Oculus Rift + Touch, the HTC Vive, and more.
- The Blueprint Visual Scripting language allows non-coders to develop game features and prototypes without the need for a programmer.
- Unreal Engine is capable of high-end materials and shaders, thus providing your players with incredibly immersive experiences.

 We will be using the latest version of the Unreal Engine for our sample project. At the time of writing this book, this version is 4.20.2. During the course of your game's development, new versions of the engine may become available. It is up to you whether to update your project to the latest version. Make this decision by looking at the release notes provided with each new version and see whether the new features will benefit your game.

What types of VR Technology are available to developers?

Knowing that Unreal Engine 4 works with the vast majority of VR technology, our next step is to choose the type of VR headset we would like to use. There are many factors that can contribute to this decision. The first is knowing who the target audience for our experience will be. Start by researching previous games that are similar to our design. By doing so, we can find out what segment of gamers will purchase our style of game and see whether we can interview a few players who fit this demographic. With this information, we can make informed design decisions as we go through the process of development, which will result in a game that really appeals to its player base.

Understanding the demographics as well as the likes and dislikes of your player base is an essential part of designing a commercially successful video game. It is also the first step in the Human-Centered Design process, a creative approach to problem solving that always keeps the user's needs and wants central to design decisions. Have a look at `https:/ /www.ideo.com/` and `dschool.stanford.edu` for more information.

The next factor we need to be aware of is what type of experience our design is most suited for. VR experiences fall into a few distinct categories:

- Room-scale VR
- Seated VR
- Mobile VR

Room-scale VR

The first is room-scale experiences.

These are active experiences that require the player to move, jump, and perform actions inside a predetermined area covered by sensors. An example of the room scale pay space covered by the lighthouse sensors that come with HTC Vive is as follows:

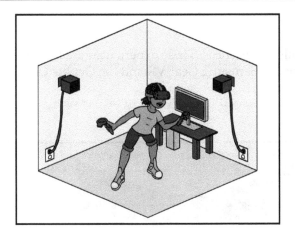

Room-scale VR

Seated VR

For experiences that may not require that particular level of activity, there are seated VR experiences. An example of the space needed for a seated-or standing-only VR experience is as follows:

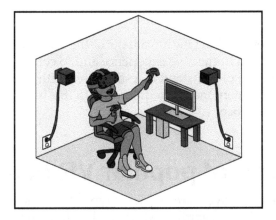

Seated VR experience

Seated experiences are built around the idea that the player remains stationary and that only the headset's orientation data is needed.

Mobile VR

Finally, there are mobile experiences. These experiences are formatted specifically for mobile devices, such as the Samsung Gear VR and the Oculus Go. The original version can be found on the following

```
link: https://commons.wikimedia.org/wiki/File:Samsung_Gear_VR_Experience_(16241
072054).jpg.
```

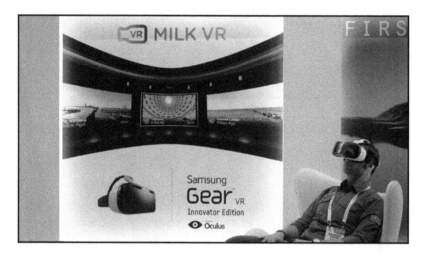

Mobile experience

Mobile experiences are designed to take advantage of the accelerator and gyroscope found in smartphones to provide an immersive experience and to control gameplay. For our game, we will likely have the player stand in a small area with their tools for the task close at hand, though some movement may be required. With this in mind, we will design *Server 17* to be a room-scale experience.

Pros and cons of popular VR headsets

Now that we know who our players are and what type of experience we want them to have, we can make the decision regarding which VR headset we would like to use to design our experience. Each type of VR headset brings different strengths and weaknesses to our project, along with specific requirements for the computer that will be running it. Let's take a look at some of the most popular VR headsets available today:

- HTC Vive
- Oculus Rift + Touch

- Windows Mixed Reality headsets
- Samsung Gear VR

HTC Vive

Released in April 2016, the HTC Vive system consists of the following:

- VR headset
- 2 x Vive motion controller
- 2 x infrared sensors, known as lighthouses

Great for room-scale experiences due to its 16ft x 16ft maximum size play area, the Vive is one of the two most popular VR systems available today, accounting for 45% of all SteamVR players in February 2018. Capable of a resolution of 2,160 x 1,200 (1,080 x 1,200 per eye), this is the headset of choice for many developers. The motion controllers can be tracked to the millimeter, and each offers nine different buttons that can be mapped inside Unreal Engine 4, which provides developers with a significant number of input options. Audio is provided by the player plugging in their own headphones, though a separate Deluxe Audio Strap may be purchased to provide a more comfortable distribution of weight and integrated headphones.

Minimum hardware requirements

- Intel Core i5-4590/AMD FX 8350 equivalent or greater
- Nvidia GeForce GTX 970/AMD Radeon R9 290 equivalent or greater
- 4 GB of RAM
- HDMI 1.4, DisplayPort 1.2 or newer
- 1x USB 2.0 or newer
- Windows 7 SP1, Winodws 8.1 or later, Windows 10

It is worth noting that while the HTC Vive is compatible with Unreal Engine 4, SteamVR is required to be running during use. With its excellent tracking, solid resolution, and flexible motion controllers, the HTC Vive is an excellent option for room-scale and seated VR experiences.

Oculus Rift + Touch

The original Oculus Rift headset was released in March 2016 by Oculus VR, after a successful Kickstarter campaign. Due to its status as a crowdfunded project, the Oculus Rift has the interesting distinction of having had its development heavily publicized. The company released two different development kits (DK1 and DK2) to its backers during development, before releasing the first commercial version. The current version of the headset includes the following:

- Oculus Rift headset
- 2 x desktop-based infrared sensors
- 2 x Oculus Touch controllers

These controllers have six different button inputs that are tracked by Unreal, but their real claim to fame is the fact that these controllers are capable of finger tracking and hand gestures. The Rift has a resolution of 2,160 x 1,200 (1,080 x 1,200 per eye), exactly the same as the HTC Vive.

Minimum hardware requirements

- Intel i3-6100/AMD Ryzen 3 1200, FX4350 or greater
- Nvidia GTX 960/AMD Radeon RX 470 or greater
- 8 GB+ of RAM
- Compatible HDMI 1.3
- 1 x USB 3.0 port and 2x USB 2.0 ports
- Windows 10

Similar to the HTC Vive, the Oculus Rift + Touch requires its own application running in the background to be able to operate. Though the Rift comes with two sensors, its recommended room scale play area is 5ft x 5ft. Though much smaller than the Vive but with the Rift's decreased hardware requirements, it is still an excellent option for seated and room-scale experiences.

Windows Mixed Reality headset

With an impressive resolution of 2,880 x 1,440 (1,440 x 1,440 per eye), the latest crop of Windows Mixed Reality headsets currently being manufactured by Acer, Lenovo, HP, and others, have the potential to really shake up the VR landscape. These headsets have integrated motion tracking to decrease setup time and potentially increase the room-scale play space available to a gamer. Their lower price compared to Vive and Oculus is also an attractive feature. However, even now, they are a new and unproven technology. The integrated motion tracking may seem like a time-saving feature, but this requires that the player is looking at whatever they want to interact with to get a smooth interaction. For developers attempting to develop the next big VR blockbuster, this is an issue that cannot be overlooked, since player experience is everything. In the end, Windows Mixed Reality hardware brings much-needed variety to the VR hardware market, but it may be too new to choose as a platform for development just yet.

Minimum hardware requirements

- Intel Core i5-7200U or greater
- Intel HD Graphics 620 or greater/DX12 capable GPU
- HDMI 1.4 or DisplayPort 1.2
- 1 x USB 3.0 Type-A or Type-C
- Windows 10 Fall Creators Update

Samsung Gear VR

The Gear VR represents the fusion of smartphone and VR technology in a sleek little package. The most recent version of this device allows the user to snap a Samsung Gear phone into a sleek frame and enjoy a variety of VR titles built specifically for the device. Controls are handled by inputs on the side of the headset, as well as by a handheld motion controller, reminiscent of those that ship with the Vive. This gives the player a variety of comfortable input options and precision controller motions. So, what does this mean for developers? The mobile CPU and 4 GB of RAM limit the ability of this device to run high-end content, but the Gear VR sports an impressive resolution of 2,560 x 1,440 (2,960 x 1,440 with Samsung Gear S8 and S8 Plus phones). The Gear VR also represents an underserved market. Though its hardware may be small, Unreal Engine 4 has supported development for the Samsung Gear VR since version 4.7, and this device is by far one of the best available for developing mobile experiences. For the savvy developer looking to build small applications, this may be a great opportunity.

Limitations of VR

Though VR is capable of delivering immersive, visceral, digital experiences to players, it is important to note that it is not without its limitations. Beyond all the RAM, processing power, sensors, cords, and controllers that VR demands, this technology has shown us some of our own limitations—the most well-known of these being VR sickness or the disconnect between what our vision is showing us and what the rest of our senses are perceiving. Most commonly felt during movement within a VR game, VR sickness, or simulation sickness, may cause any of the following:

- Nausea
- Dizziness
- Disorientation
- Sweating
- Various other ailments

All of these things are things we don't wish to be a part of any player's experience. These can be caused by features within games that we sometimes take for granted in a non-virtual environment, such as taking control away from the player to show them a cutscene, using camera bob, camera shake, or overriding the player's field of view. Issues can also can arise from the framerate dropping too low. For this reason, we as developers must be constantly aware of our game's performance on our chosen platform. In the following screenshot, we have the recommended framerates for several of the VR headsets that Unreal Engine 4 supports:

HMD Device	Target Frame Rate
DK1	60 FPS
DK2	75 FPS
Rift Retail	90 FPS
Vive	90 FPS
Gear VR	60 FPS
PSVR	Variable up to 120 FPS

Unreal Engine 4's VR recommended framerates, courtesy of Epic Games

Choosing a method of locomotion and turning that provides the player with a constant and steady feeling of acceleration, and is just one way to do this. Some established methods of locomotion that have arisen from development in VR techniques include cockpit-based, natural, artificial, physical, and teleportation. We will learn more about these methods of locomotion and how they might suit our game in Chapter 2, *Locomotion, Design, and Starting Our Project*. Other methods of controlling VR sickness include avoiding cinematic camera effects that alter the player's vision, such as motion blur and using dimmer lighting. Bright colors and blurring effects will cause players nausea as a result of eye strain. Finally, it is also worth noting that medical science has still not thoroughly studied the effects of the prolonged use of VR, as well as the issues that might arise from children regularly using the device. As designers, player experience should always be at the front of our minds, and keeping our players from being physically uncomfortable is one of the most important ways we can keep them coming back to our game.

Introducing our sample project – Server 17

To help frame our exploration of VR development with Unreal Engine 4, we will develop a game I like to call *Server 17*. Designed as a room-scale experience geared toward gamers who enjoy VR and skill-based games, *Server 17* puts players in the shoes of a cyberpunk hacker in a dystopian future of corrupt governments and mega corporations. The player will have to unlock the secrets of a corporate server, which will be represented in game as a puzzle box. They will have access to a variety of tools and programs that will allow them to succeed before network security can catch them in the act and bring them down.

 For this project, I have chosen to use Unreal Engine 4 with the HTC Vive. The Vive gives our players a nice, large room-space experience with excellent tracking of both the headset and the hand controllers. It also utilizes less USB ports on the computer. This is a great feature, since I am developing on a high-end laptop with limited ports. Though it does not have the finger tracking you may find with the Oculus Rift + Touch, it is an excellent piece of hardware that will meet the needs of this project.

Summary

As we take our first steps down the road to becoming VR developers, we took a look at the decisions that we will have to make before getting started with developing our first VR title. We also took a look at several compelling reasons to choose Unreal Engine 4, such as continual support for VR, free access, Blueprint Visual Scripting, and powerful shader tools. We then discussed the different types of VR experiences that currently exist and which type of hardware might suit itself best to each one. Finally, we discussed VR sickness and how this debilitating condition can best be avoided.

As we move onto Chapter 2, *Locomotion, Design, and Starting Our Project*, we will make some decisions about how best to design our sample game, *Server 17*, and we will create the necessary setup files to start moving forward with development. To make sure we all understand how each of the blueprint files interact, I will be creating as much of the content as I can from scratch, only using templates and premade files when needed. Welcome to the adventure—let's move forward!

2
Locomotion, Design, and Starting Our Project

With our knowledge of the current state of VR technology and game development, we may now begin working on our first title. As we mentioned in Chapter 1, *Introducing VR Technology in Unreal Engine 4*, *Server 17* puts the player in the role of an intrepid hacker in search of the truth in a corrupt dystopian future. Everyone has secrets, and some will pay big sums of money for the secrets of others. In design terms, this means we're going to create a puzzle game in which the player solves puzzles and uses different tools to crack open different puzzle boxes that represent computer servers on a network. Through the building of this simple game, we'll address all of the steps of VR game design with the goal of arming you with the tools and know-how to begin work on your own title. The first step in the process is design and, for that, I always turn to the Human-Centered Design process.

In this chapter, we'll cover the following topics:

- The Human-Centered Design process
- Choosing our locomotion method
- Setting up new game files in Unreal Engine 4
- Project setup

The Human-Centered Design process

The **Human-Centered Design** (HCD) process is a flexible set of design principles that allows for the design of pretty much anything, from shoes, to cars, to software. Central to HCD is the principle that the designer is thinking of the end user at every step of the way. Would this decision make the product better for my user? Would making the color customizable delight my user and make them more likely to use my product? By asking these questions and thinking about your user, you're able to create a design that's more likely to be a success with its target audience.

The HCD process has the following steps:

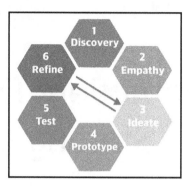

The HCD process

1. **Discovery**: In this, we research the problem we're presented with and the target demographic interested in our solution. We search to see whether this is something that someone has attempted to solve before and if so what they tried. We reach out to our potential users to find people who will talk to us so we can discover what they need from a solution.

2. **Empathy**: Here, we speak with as many potential users as possible to gather what they're looking for in a solution. We want to dig deep. Why is this something they want or need? Are there any connections back to a memory or an emotion? For example, nostalgia is a powerful longing for experiences related to a person's youth. It's also one of the strongest emotions that game developers like to touch on.

3. **Ideate**: Once we know what our user wants, it's time to brainstorm! When we ideate, we want to come up with as many ideas as possible. No idea is too out there or crazy (as long as it benefits our user).

4. **Prototype**: Once we settle on an idea, we want to build a quick and easy version to allow our user to try it. No fancy programming or incredible art here—we want to create a playable version of our game, quickly and cheaply.

5. **Test**: Put the prototype in front of the user and record the results! It's often at this point that a product may fail. This might be caused by a problem with the design or something that the user didn't understand or like. Record the data and learn from it!

6. **Refine**: With the user test data in hand, we go back to the ideate phase and try again. You'll likely go through this cycle several times before your game is complete, but if you're checking in with your user regularly and getting feedback from other designers and friends, you'll surely come up with the next killer app.

For *Server 17*, our ideal user is someone who has never experienced VR before. They're interested in a simple, yet very immersive experience that leverages the unique abilities of VR. They may be fans of cyberpunk movies such as *Tron* and *Tron: Legacy* and the *Shadowrun* series of games. Nostalgia may also come into play when they think about their first experience with a new piece of gaming hardware. It's possible you have many friends who fit this profile that you can use as a reference while designing the game and we can also make use of online communities to gather further opinions. Once we've completed the **Discovery** and **Empathy** steps with a bit of research and some interviews with our user, we're now ready to make a few design decisions regarding locomotion, or the process of our player moving through our game world.

Choosing our locomotion method

One of our goals as VR designers is to leverage the unique advantages of this new technology to create novel experiences that players want to play again and again. The technology is fantastic for making the player feel as if they're interacting in a living and breathing fantasy world they would otherwise not be able to inhabit. Using the hand controllers, our players can touch our world and interact with it in a very visceral sense. However, locomotion systems still haven't caught up to that level of immersion yet.

Player locomotion in VR is still in its infancy, and, as such, there's no one method that has been found to work well. Many methods have been tried. There are vehicle simulation games, where the player remains seated in a cockpit. There are action/adventure games where players run through a landscape using artificial methods such as a thumbstick or teleportation. Others attempt to maintain immersion by having the player stand within a small area with everything they need readily accessible, allowing the player to move around naturally but at the expense of an expansive environment. Each method of locomotion is a trade-off between giving the player an immersive, natural sensation and avoiding unpleasant feelings, such as VR sickness.

During my time as a college professor, I had the opportunity to help my students to design a kayaking simulator for the local museum. The students devised a locomotion system that allowed the player to remain seated and use a paddle with an attached sensor to navigate their virtual craft down the river rapids. Though the system worked well in testing with their peers (it felt natural and worked well for me), we found that it had a profoundly negative affect on several of our users at the museum. One of our testers even had to leave work after testing our game. After asking the tester some questions, it was discovered that, although the paddle movement of our controller felt right, the realistic physics of the boat in the water made it impossible for them to play. Further questioning of the test group showed the students that this one tester wasn't the only player who had issues. In the end, they had to take some artistic license with the movement of the water to create a more enjoyable experience and learned that our user's experience and enjoyment was more important than realism.

While this lack of a best practice may be concerning to some, the designer in us all should see this as an exciting opportunity to innovate and create new systems that provide our players with the best gameplay possible. The variety of systems can be broken down into four major categories:

- Natural
- Artificial
- Cockpit
- Physical (creative)

Natural locomotion

Not to be confused with the app of the same name, natural locomotion refers to a method of moving within VR that minimizes VR sickness by taking natural player movements, such as swinging arms and jumping, into the game world. We can see natural locomotion at work in the game *Tribe XR* as follows:

Tribe XR is an up and coming DJ app that can teach you how to mix music with in-game lessons

This covers a variety of methods, but all seem to provide the player with a direct translation of their movement into player movement in the game. Though this method has been shown to limit player discomfort, it isn't without its drawbacks. This approach limits the player to the space covered by their system's sensors and requires designers to design with this in mind. This can mean designing the level specifically around the average playspace size and making sure that everything the player needs is well within reach. This method has been used in such games as *Job Simulator*, *Tribe VR*, and *Waltz of the Wizard*.

Artificial locomotion

Artificial locomotion is essentially the opposite of natural locomotion. This technique relies on more traditional game controls such as thumbsticks, touch pads, and other input methods to move the player around our game levels.

Despite being the best locomotion when porting traditional titles to VR (think *Skyrim VR* and *Fallout 4 VR*), artificial locomotion has the greatest chance of causing VR sickness due to vexation, or the disconnect between what our eyes are seeing and what the rest of the senses are experiencing. There are several techniques we can use to minimize this vexation. One way is to dynamically decrease the player's field of view while they're moving. This creates a very subtle effect that hides some of the player's peripheral vision when they're moving or turning. Another is to have the player accelerate at a consistent rate during movement. Consistent acceleration puts less pressure on the vestibular system—the portion of our brain that senses acceleration. The same principle can be applied to rotation. Consistent slow turning or snap turning can feel better to a player. The final technique I would like to mention is teleportation. Teleportation is a great way to allow a player to navigate large environments without VR sickness. However, this method doesn't feel very natural depending on the game's story and setting.

Cockpit locomotion

Similar to natural locomotion, cockpit locomotion allows for very natural movement for games such as space sims, vehicle racing, and other games that have the player sitting in a vehicle.

By tricking the body into thinking that movement is similar to riding in a car, we can bypass many of the causes of VR sickness. The downside to this method is that it isn't applicable to most situations. Games that use this method successfully include *Elite: Dangerous, Star Trek Bridge Crew*, and *Archangel: Hellfire*.

Physical locomotion

Physical locomotion systems refer to unique movement control schemes that tend to be designed for the specific game experiences they're applied to. Because of this, they tend to be some of the most innovative ideas that we see in the VR space today.

This type of locomotion covers purpose built movement methods such as the kayak paddle system built by my students, as well as hand-over-hand climbing, running in place while swinging the controllers, swimming motions, and flying by moving the player's arms. Because the player is making specific arm or body movements, they tend to feel a very high rate of immersion while experiencing very little VR sickness. These systems aren't without disadvantages. Some players may find the movement silly or gimmicky. They're also not usually usable outside their specific game. Games that have successfully implemented this type of locomotion include *The Climb, Eagle Flight*, and the spell casting mechanic found in *Waltz of the Wizard*.

Taking into account what we know about our user (new to VR, looking for immersive and visceral experiences, and fans of cyberpunk), what type or types of locomotion would be best here? For the new user, natural locomotion seems as though it would work the best, since it tends to be intuitive and works well for maintaining immersion. So that we aren't limiting our level design to just the player's defined play space, we can also choose to integrate teleportation into our control scheme. Despite its drawback of not being immersive, I feel that the cyberspace setting of our game would actually support the player teleporting around the level.

With these design decisions made, it's time to launch **Unreal Engine 4 (UE4)** and set up our project files!

Setting up new game files in UE4

UE4 is a versatile collection of tools that helps you to create the game of your dreams. To get you started down that path, Epic Games provides a collection of starter projects to jump-start your games by setting up some of the most important features for you. This often includes player character, sample weapons, and other necessary files. In this book, we'll begin creating files within the Virtual Reality Starter project so that we can make use of some of the basic art assets that this project provides. Beyond that, I'll show you how to create the blueprints we'll need from scratch.

 Every game or software project needs to stay organized and we use **naming conventions** to do just that. A naming convention is a naming scheme and folder structure that ensures that every filename is standardized so that anyone in a particular game team can read a filename and understand exactly what they're looking at. You may have noticed it while browsing through some of the project files inside UE4. Epic Games provides its naming convention on the Unreal Wiki at `https://wiki.unrealengine.com/Assets_Naming_Convention`, and we'll be using it throughout this book.

Any new game in Unreal needs certain blueprints created to customize the project to fit our needs. These files include the following:

- `GameMode`
- `GameState`
- `PlayerPawn`

But how do all of these files interact, and why do we need them? When UE4 launches a game, the engine creates two files to help it understand what the rules of the game are before it loads and levels or players. These are `GameMode` and `GameState`. `GameMode` contains the rules that make our game unique, such as the total number of players and how those players connect to the game, as well as default settings, such as the default player pawn, player controller, and game state. By creating our own game mode, we're taking the first step toward customizing our project. The `GameState` file that's loaded after the game starts is designed to track everything that's important to our game, such as scores, missions completed, and other elements that are relevant to the game as a whole. This isn't for things that are player-specific, as there is a different player state. I've often used this as a place to store data needed to build levels in a procedural generation game, for example. Lastly, we'll need a custom `PlayerPawn`. `PlayerPawn` is the player's physical representation in the game and is possessed by our player during the game.

Project setup

Before we can start creating our custom project files, we need to let Unreal create our project base and begin to lay out our folder structure. This will keep our files organized as we build *Server 17*.

Start by opening Unreal Engine 4.20.2 and starting a new project:

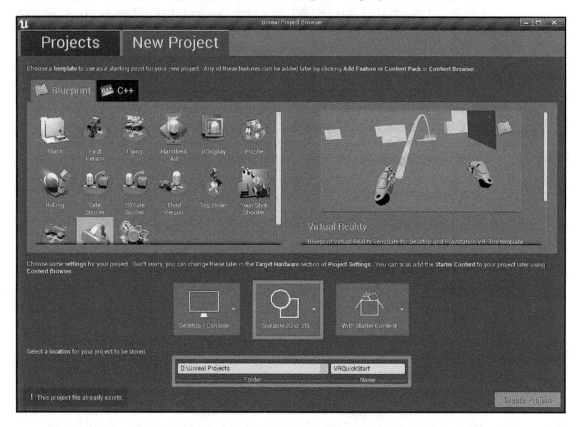

The screen you're greeted with when you first open UE4

Welcome to the new project window. From here, we'll create our project based on the UR template:

1. Choose the new project tab from the top of the screen.
2. Select the **Blueprint** section.
3. Choose the **Virtual Reality** template near the bottom of the list.

4. Change the middle project setting to **Scalable 3D or 2D**.
5. Ensure the project folder is in a space you can find easily. Change the name to VRQuickStart.

Smack that **Create Project** button, and let's continue! Now take a look at the interface:

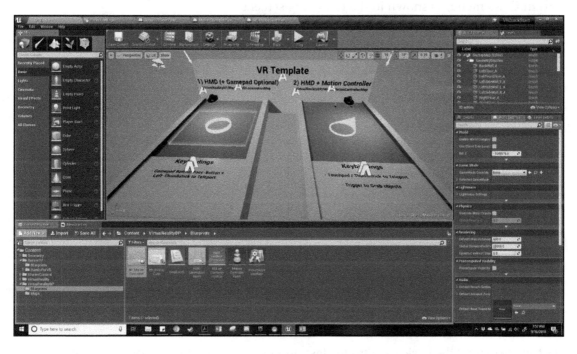

Much of the interaction with the game engine takes place in the Content Browser

With our new project open, look around the interface and locate your **Content Browser**:

1. It's time to get organized. One of the first steps is to create our own project folder similar to the VirtualReality and VirtualRealityBP folders Epic Games uses. Right-click on the Content folder inside the **Content Browser** and select **New Folder** from the top of the list. Name the new folder Server17.
2. Click on our new folder to enter it. Right-click in the **Content Browser** and select **New Folder**. Name it Blueprints. This will be the home of our new blueprints.

As we continue with development, we'll add several more folders to our file structure to help to contain and organize our files. Remember to stick to our naming convention as we go, as this will be a huge help later when you're adding team members or coming back to your project after a leave of absence.

Creating our custom Game Mode

With our project base and our file structure established, let's create our first custom file: our `GameMode` file. Click on our new `Blueprints` folder, and right-click to bring up the menu. From the **Create Basic Asset** section, choose **Blueprint Class**. This will bring up the **Pick Parent Class** menu, as shown in the following screenshot:

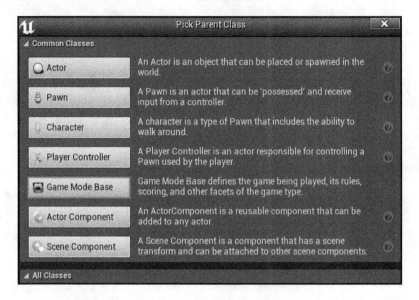

From the Pick Parent Class menu, we can create a new file that extends the functionality of a parent file

It's time to extend the basic `GameMode` class and tell our project to use our new file:

1. From the **Pick Parent Class** menu, we can extend any basic class that the engine has to offer. Click the **Game Mode Base** button, and name the new file `S17GameMode`.

2. Simply creating `GameMode` isn't enough for the engine to recognize it within our project. To ensure that it's used, click on the **Settings** button of the viewport and select **Project settings**.

Alternately, we could have opened up the **World Settings** and navigated down to the **Game Mode** section of the menu, and then clicked the + button next to the **GameMode Override**. Much like doing math or most creative pursuits, there's more than one way to create something inside Unreal. What I'm sharing are the methods and processes that I've learned in my career. If you find a different way or a better way to do any of the things that I talk about in this book, feel free to share them with me and the UE4 development community!

Check out the **Project settings** menu:

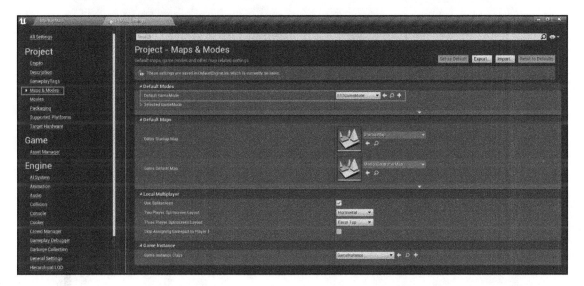

Project settings

3. Under the **Project** section of the menu, select **Maps & Modes**. This section of the menu allows you to specify the default map that opens when the editor opens, as well as define the default GameMode.

4. In the **Default Modes** section of the menu, use the **Default GameMode** drop-down menu and select **S17GameMode**.

With the **S17GameMode** set as our default, we can now begin to create the rest of our custom project files. We'll come back to the **Projects** setting screen and change the defaults further once we have the rest of our pieces in place.

Creating a GameState

Where `GameMode` is great for setting our game specific rules and storing our mode defaults, `GameState` is there to store our important level-wide elements. Similar to when we created our `GameMode` class, we'll need to extend a `GameState` class as the base for our custom state. Let's go back to the **Pick Parent Class** menu:

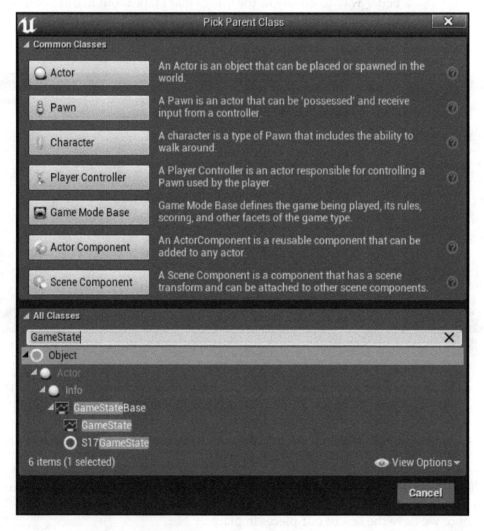

Extending GameStateBase to create our custom GameState class

Yet, unlike our `GameMode`, we're going to extend the `GameStateBase` class, or the class from which all `GameState` files extend:

1. Right-click in the **Content Browser** and select the **Blueprint Class** from the **Create Basic Asset** section of the menu.
2. From the **Pick Parent Class** menu, we're going to skip the top portion of the menu that lists many of the common extended classes and select the **All Classes** collapsed menu.
3. This will show us all of the classes that we can extend within the engine. Use the search box to find the **GameStateBase** and select it. Then, press the **Select** button at the bottom of the menu.
4. Name our new game state `S17GameState`.

A discussion of the interaction between `GameMode`, `GameState`, and individual `PlayerStates` in the context of single and multiplayer games.

Creating a custom PlayerPawn

Now that we have two different files to help with managing the information and variables that will be present in our level, it's time to build our `PlayerPawn`, or the physical representation of our player. `PlayerPawn` takes in information from the headset and hand controllers and translates that into movement and action within the game. Depending on how we choose to represent our player, there are several different directions we can go in:

- **First-person format**: The player has no avatar. The hands and head float in the air.
- **First person with arms**: Using inverse kinematics, we're able to give the player arms that move with the location of the hand controllers. However, the head still floats.

- **First person with full body**: Similar to the first person with arms setup, this allows the player to be represented by a full body, with inverse kinematics used for both the hands and the head.
- **Third person**: A full third-person character with the player looking down on it from a camera set above and behind the player model. This option has been known to limit VR sickness but at the cost of immersion. This player setup has been successfully used in some games when used in conjunction with a first-person option—for example: the first-person view is used when the player is shooting and performing actions, but the third-person view is used when the player is moving.

For *Server 17*, the player takes on the role of a cyberpunk hacker trying to break into a server to find encrypted file data to steal. Set in the future, and the player and the server interact inside a virtual environment created by the player's hacking hardware. For this reason, we can represent the player using the basic first-person format without sacrificing the experience. This method will also help with keeping our game optimized.

Though we could use the Motion Controller Pawn that's supplied with the template we're using, let's go ahead and create one from scratch. Start by creating a new `Pawn` class for us to use:

1. Right-click in the **Content Browser** within our `Blueprints` folder and select **Blueprint Class** from the **New Basic Asset** section of the menu.
2. We want to create a new **Pawn** for our player to possess or to receive controller input data. Select **Pawn** from the menu and name it `S17PlayerPawn`. Double-click the new **Pawn** to open the interface, as follows:

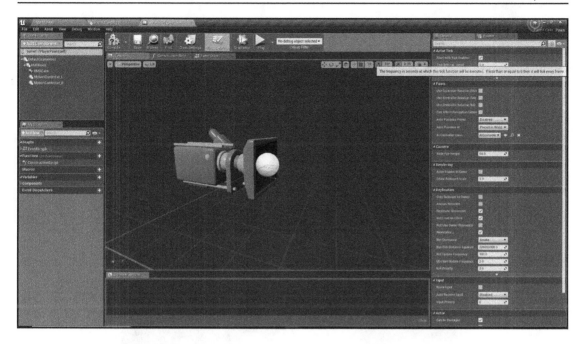

The open Pawn class with components showing

3. First, we'll add a scene component to our player to act as a root object for our camera. In the top-left of the **Blueprint** interface, in the **Components** panel of the menu, click on the **Add Component** button and search for a **Scene Component**. Create it and name it HMDRoot.

4. It's time to add our player camera as a child of our new **Scene** object. With HMDRoot selected, go back to the **Add Component** button and find a **Camera** object. Create it and name it HMDCam.

5. Now we need to create a way to track our player's motion controllers so that the hands of our player character move and act appropriately. With HMDRoot selected, create a **Motion Controller** component with the **Add Component** menu and name it MotionController_L.

6. Repeat the preceding steps to create another **Motion Controller** component and name it `MotionController_R`. The **Details** panel will look like this:

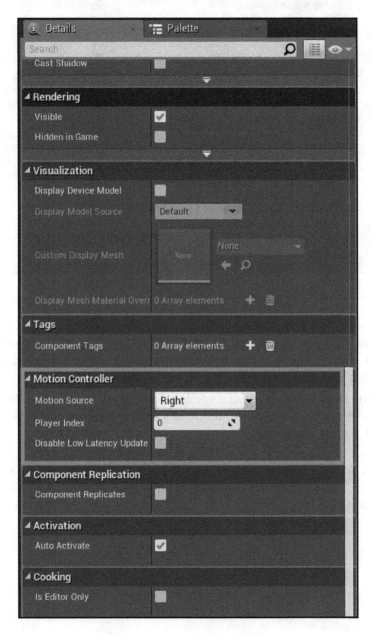

MotionController_R settings

7. With our MotionController_R component selected, look over at the **Details** panel and find the **Motion Controller** section of the menu. Change the **Motion Source** option to **Right**.

Programming our custom PlayerPawn

Let's move on to a bit of programming to ensure that our PlayerPawn is used and set up correctly for our player's hardware. Unreal needs to know where to set the Tracking Origin, or where to set the default height of the player, which can vary depending on your equipment. For the HTC Vive, the default is to target standing VR experiences by using a tracking origin set to the floor. The Oculus Rift, on the other hand, is set to target sitting VR experiences by default and uses an eye-level tracking origin. It might be easy to simply just set things up for the Vive, knowing that this is the platform we're targeting, but I want to create something that might be reusable outside just this project. We'll add the following to our PlayerPawn's Event Graph:

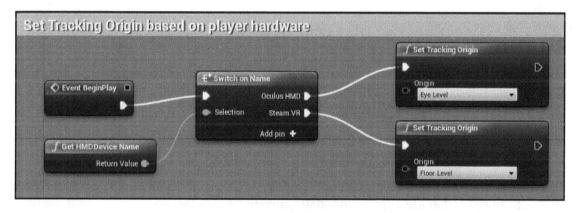

PlayerPawn Event Graph

To do this, we'll detect what hardware the player might be using and set the Tracking Origin based on our player's equipment:

1. Click on the **Event Graph** tab in the center of our S17PlayerPawn and drag an execute line out of the **Event BeginPlay** node.
2. Drop it and select the **Switch on Name** node. **Switch on Name** is a flow-control node, which means that it restricts and directs the flow of execution through the blueprint. This node will direct the blueprint to set the tracking origin based on the HMD hardware found.

3. Drag off the **Selection** input on the **Switch on Name** node. Use the search box to find **Get HMD Device Name**. This node represents a function designed to fetch the name of the player's HMD hardware.

4. On the **Switch on Name** node, click the **Add Pin** button two times. In the **Details** panel, name the pins **OculusHMD** and **SteamVR**. Also in the **Details** panel, turn off the option has **Default Pin**.

5. Now let's set the criteria for each of our hardware options. Drag off the **OculusHMD** pin and search for the **Set Tracking Origin** node. Select it, and use the drop-down box on the node to select **Eye Level** tracking.

6. Drag off the **SteamVR** pin, and create another **Set Tracking** origin node. This time, we'll set it to **Floor Level** tracking.

7. Now click the **Save** button, so you don't lose your work.

With our tracking origin in place, we can now go back into our project settings and tell S17GameMode to use our S17PlayerPawn as our Default Player Pawn.

Summary

At the beginning of this chapter, we learned one of the best ways to design with a particular type of user in mind: the HCD process. When using HCD, we always want to keep our player in mind as we make each design decision, ensuring that the game we create meets every one of our player's expectations and is a delight to play. This is our goal for *Server 17*. With a few of our design decisions in place, we then created our project and began to customize our files by creating our custom GameMode, GameState, and PlayerPawn files.

In the next chapter, we'll further flesh out the design for *Server 17* and look at the different types of gameplay that are popular in today's current VR market. Specifically, we'll focus on gameplay that takes advantage of the unique input methods and immersive qualities that VR has to offer and how we can apply those to our own game. In the end, we'll decide how our game will work and begin building those systems. Soon, we'll have a working prototype that we can show off to our players!

Exploring Riveting Gameplay in Virtual Reality

3

With our custom game files in place, it's time to start making some decisions about gameplay. In *Server 17*, the player takes on the role of a futuristic hacker trying to crack open a corporate server and plunder its secrets for personal gain. So, how might we present this in VR as an experience? Before we think about that, let's do a bit of research and discovery. The best way to learn which mechanics will challenge and entertain our players is to first look at the unique elements that VR brings to a game. After that, we can take a look at which titles are being played right now and why. Armed with that information, we can then make some decisions about how best to design our own gameplay for *Server 17*. We have a lot to discover, so let's get started!

In this chapter, we'll cover the following topics:

- What does VR bring to video games?
- Popular gameplay mechanics
- Designing the gameplay for *Server 17*

What does VR bring to video games?

VR is the new frontier in games and entertainment. It's able to put the player in the shoes of their favorite heroes, or in a front-row seat for some of their favorite experiences. In most experiences, player movement is translated into near one-to-one movement inside the game—something that's usually impossible in traditional video games. VR also has the power to immerse our player in an alternate world and make them truly feel as if they're there. It's these special abilities that mark VR as the future of gaming.

It's important to understand that the input and controls in VR can go beyond the locomotion methods that we discussed in the last chapter. Each controller for the Vive or Oculus brings at least six different buttons that can be mapped to different functions within a game. Each of these can then be combined with a location or specific player movement to create almost infinite variety. Let's take a look at some of the gunplay in Epic Game's *Robo Recall*.

In this game, you destroy robots with a variety of weapons that are holstered on the player. The character has a pair of pistols holstered at their hips and a second pair of weapons holstered at their shoulders. This seems simple enough, right? Where the designers utilized the advantages of VR was in the hand placement needed to use your weapons. The player has to reach down to their waist to grab a pistol or reach behind their shoulder to grab a weapon. This simple addition of hand location to the input to equip a gun adds to the immersion and visceral quality of the gameplay.

Popular gameplay mechanics

In the last few years, many developers have embraced VR technology as their chosen medium. This has lead to a variety of VR games spanning many different genres and ideas. Each game has approached the input and immersion that VR brings in their own way. Some, such as Bethesda and ID Software, chose to use the technology to bring their blockbuster games *Fallout 4* and *Doom* into the VR era (to mixed reviews). Others have found more success building their game specifically for the medium, such as Beat Games' *Beat Saber*, and Schell Games' *I Expect You To Die*. For our research into what might work for *Server 17*, we're going to look at seven different types of gameplay:

- Shooter experiences
- Action/adventure experiences
- Vehicle experiences
- Physics-based experiences
- Puzzle experiences
- Rhythm experiences
- Educational experiences

Shooter experiences

In the last year, more than a dozen of the top 25 VR titles sold on Valve's Steam download service fell into the shooter category. A shooter is defined as any game that includes gunplay as a major part of experience. Many variations on the shooter experience in VR take advantage of unique mechanics. Still near the top of the charts is *Robo Recall*.

Epic Games was able to combine the frantic action of a wave shooter with the immersive environment and mechanics that VR can bring. Much of the gameplay centers around using your hands. *Robo Recall* uses interesting mechanics when it comes to arming yourself. Players grab their chosen weapons from holsters located at their waist and shoulders. Each one is filled with a variety of customized weapons, all great for scrapping the game's robot enemies. The grab mechanism is also applied to a specific brand of melee combat from *Robo Recall*. Player's can grab many robot enemies by a handle that's conveniently located in the center of their chest. Once grabbed, enemies can be ripped apart by grabbing limbs, thrown into other enemies, or held up as shields to protect yourself.

Superhot VR by Superhot Team is another game that takes gunplay to a whole new level. The game combines physics and shooting gameplay with their exclusive time mechanics to create a rare experience. Just about every object in its minimalist environments is a weapon in *Superhot VR*. These items can be thrown at an enemy to liberate their weapon, causing it to fly into the air so that it can be snatched up by the player. Combined with the fact that time only moves forward when you do, each level becomes a combat puzzle. Which enemy do you confront first? What weapon or object is available within arm's reach? Each decision and movement is important for discovering the level's solution, and progressing.

The most important elements of a popular VR shooter are active gunplay combined with another unique mechanic. This can be grabbing, physics gameplay, or a particular locomotion mechanism. Other great examples in this category include *Sairento VR*, for its locomotion mechanic and combination of gun and swordplay, as well as *Damaged Core*, a game that has the player utilizing the ability to teleport from enemy to enemy, possessing them and using their weapons.

Action/adventure experiences

Action/adventure experiences combine combat experiences with exploration and story-based gameplay. These games feature impressive environments and visuals that take advantage of the fact that VR places the player directly into the game world. Yet, with such a large world in which to explore, designers must use artificial locomotion methods to allow the player to explore such a large space. For many players, the ability to experience the story firsthand outweighs any discomfort caused by using a thumbstick or snap turning for locomotion. In this category, the biggest contenders both come to us from *Bethesda Softworks : Fallout 4 VR and Skyrim VR.*

Fallout 4 VR is a direct port of the popular 2015 title, redesigned to work with VR. Players travel the wasteland building settlements, crafting equipment, and experiencing the story from a first-person perspective. Combat is an in-your-face affair. The majority of the early enemies favor close combat, meaning there isn't much of a chance for the player to use a firearm before their opponent is right on top of them. Luckily, melee combat is as simple as equipping the right weapon, or none at all, and swinging away. Ranged combat also feels good, though not nearly as satisfying as in a VR shooter. Still, *Fallout 4* ticks all of the right boxes. It's an action/adventure experience that gives players a massive, awe-inspiring environment. In it, they may craft, build, and interact, as well as take part in a deep story with a variety of interesting characters.

Vehicle experiences

Vehicle experiences solve the locomotion problem by placing the player at the helm of a ship, mech, or other method of travel and destruction. The brain processes it much the same as when we go for a ride in the car. We don't question that we're moving because we're sitting down and controlling the vehicle. This gives the designers the opportunity to give players a vehicle-piloting experience. There are many great examples in this space. However, I want to give you one that represents some of the best gameplay in this category, Frontier Developments' *Elite Dangerous*.

The most current entry in the *Elite* saga is a space adventure, combat, and trading sim that puts the player in the role of an elite commander. Players earn money, rank, and influence with the major factions of a one-to-one, open-world version of our Milky Way galaxy. The game can be played without VR hardware, but it truly shines when the player dons the headgear. When played in VR, the player is able to see the inside of the ship and see their own customized player character sitting at the helm.

Navigating the systems and menus of the ship becomes easier as menus open with a glance. Combat and piloting become effortless, since the player can look through the canopy of their ship to help track their location. All of these VR-specific features add depth to an amazing experience as the players fight, trade, and explore their way to fortune and fame within the game world.

The addition of an internal ship environment, customizable player character, and eye tracking-based menus are only possible thanks to the first-person perspective that VR provides. Being able to see themselves in the interior of their vehicle connects the player to their surroundings. This makes them feel as if they're a living part of the game. Whether it's racing in a tricked-out high-performance street car or fighting aliens in the depths of space, the player's vehicle-piloting experience is enhanced by the VR perspective.

Physics-based experiences

Not as well known in the gaming world, physics-based games take advantage of the player's ability to aim and throw objects using a standing or room-space experience. This goes beyond simply picking up and throwing everyday objects, such as the gameplay found in *Superhot VR*. It takes advantage of a game engine's ability to simulate real-world physics to create gameplay. In this genre, the games tend to take the form of phyiscs-based fighting games and physics puzzle games. Let's take a look at the physics-based combat game, *Gorn*.

Gorn, from Devolver Digital, casts the player as a gladiator fighting for the amusement of several large-headed patrons. The game features cartoon-style art and violence, centered around comical physics-based brawling. Each round starts with the player entering the arena, sometimes with a selection of weapons and sometimes unarmed. The rules are simple: knock out the other guys before they do the same to you. The fun comes when the player picks a weapon to use. As the game translates their movement into the game world, it adds a bit of cartoon physics. Movements become exaggerated. Weapons feel as if they're made of foam or rubber, making combat a strange affair. Together, these features come together to create a brawling experience that feels visceral and absurd at the same time. *Gorn* is currently available for HTC Vive, Oculus Rift, and PlayStation VR.

In contrast to the fighting gameplay of *Gorn* is the physics-based puzzler, *Bounce*. *Bounce*, developed by Steel Wool Studios, has the player helping a ball-shaped robot navigate the corridors of an intergalactic spaceship. Players are given an array of physics gadgets designed to propel their robot friend from one side of the level to the exit portal. To get there, the robot must navigate around laser walls, gravity wells, and other sci-fi obstructions. Beating the game unlocks style mode. This allows the player to play each of the game's 50 levels again and rewards them for the most creative solutions.

In both games, we can again see the unique movement mechanic and first-person perspective often seen in VR, used to great effect. *Gorn* uses player arm movement with cartoon physics to create a gaming experience that feels fun and intense. In contrast, *Bounce* uses the first-person perspective to allow the player see what placing a particular physics gadget will do when the ball hits it. This gives the player the ability to see firsthand the effects of their actions and allows the player to feel more in control of the experience.

Puzzle experiences

With their use of object manipulation as a major mechanism and often fantasy environments, puzzle experiences lend themselves very well to the VR treatment. Since the time of *Myst* and it's sequels, players have shown time and again that they love solving the mysteries of ancient ruins, dark dungeons, and castles in the sky. However, until now, players haven't been able to truly reach eye level with some of these puzzles and environments, which can make solving problems where you have to aim a laser or shoot a bow much harder. Take as an example the laser puzzles from the game *The Talos Principle VR* by Croteam, a port of the popular puzzle game from 2014. Players are required in several puzzles to use a device to bend a laser beam to hit a particular target. Some players have reported that this task is considerably easier in VR due to their ability to bend down and see where the laser will travel from eye level.

Another great example of VR principles applied to puzzle gameplay can be found in the standout title *I Expect You to Die* by Schell Games. In this game, the player takes on the role of a telekinetic super spy, charged with completing various missions to defeat the evil Zoraxis Organization. Each of the five locations in the game feels a bit like an escape room. The player is given the task of escaping the area and must use the tools they find to complete the mission. For instance, the first mission of the game has the player tasked with driving the evil Dr. Zor's weaponized car out of the back of a cargo plane while the plane is slowly filling with poison gas and using only the tools found in the car or dismantled ones from the car's many attempts to kill you. The game gets around the locomotion issue by giving the player the choice of making it a sitting or room-scale experience and by giving the player telekinesis so they never have to move. Together, the game uses the uniqueness of VR and creativity to great effect to create an experience that has players singing its praises.

Rhythm experiences

In many ways, VR mechanics are breathing new life into the game genres that we love. This is especially true of rhythm games whose basic gameplay mechanics of *press this button at this time* seem old by today's standards. However, the application of VR-specific gameplay mechanics such as one-to-one arm movement have revitalized the genre and given rise to several unique rhythm experiences. At the top of that list is certainly *Beat Saber*, developed and published by Beat Games.

Beat Saber combines rhythm gameplay with VR saber combat to create a unique title that has players swinging virtual red and blue energy sabers to hit the corresponding color blocks in time with the music. Players must strike the blocks with the correct color saber at the correct angle while ducking and dodging wall obstacles and mines that shouldn't be hit. All of this action is set to the tempo of the song. With a variety of tracks and difficulty settings, *Beat Saber* sets a new standard for rhythm experiences in the age of VR. In this game, we see two types of gameplay collide: VR combat (swinging at stuff and dodging) and rhythm mechanics. The combination creates an almost dancing experience that makes it easy to enjoy. Though be prepared for a workout even if you're playing this as a seated experience, as some of the songs get very energetic at times.

Educational experiences

Since its inception, educators have been interested in VR as a way to instruct and train the next generation in a way that's engaging and allows the learner to see the material from a new perspective. New generations of students are looking for education institutions to embrace technology while providing a unique and experiential style of learning. To meet this demand, education software developers, college development teams, and even some game developers have begun creating VR experiences that allow students to experience history close up or to learn to use high-end equipment without fear of hurting themselves. Besides immersion and unique mechanics, VR can allow those who wish to learn something that takes expensive equipment or rare resources the opportunity to do so. Here are some of the titles currently available:

- *The Body VR: Journey Inside a Cell*: This game uses the immersion of VR to allow the player to experience traveling in the bloodstream of a human being and enter a blood cell to see the inner workings at the cellular level.

- *Sharecare VR*: This application allows the player to explore the anatomy of the human body, simulate disease, and show how treatment interacts with the body. Players can also call up specific organs and enable the display of tags to show specific structures. This allows players to learn and study the human anatomy in ways that weren't possible previously.
- *Apollo 11 VR*: *Apollo 11* combines a passive viewing experience with occasional mini games to allow the player to live the Apollo 11 mission firsthand.

I also want to mention *Tribe XR* here. Though the developers have chosen to teach users how to DJ using high-end equipment, the goal is to create a creative education platform that can be used to teach many skills and take advantage of what they refer to as exponential learning. As part of the plan for their platform, they're allowing vetted users, in this case other DJs, to teach those new to the platform both in recorded and live lessons. This mechanism has amazing potential for revolutionizing how schools and businesses teach and train their students.

VR has the ability to bring the user into the game worlds that we create and turn their movements into real in-game action. These two unique features have the potential to revolutionize how players enjoy video games and create new avenues for designers to express themselves creatively. However, we need to make sure that these new techniques for creating interaction within game worlds to become a crutch that props up poor design. Like the graphics advances of the early 20's, we mustn't let VR become a novelty and an excuse for bad games.

Designing the gameplay for Server 17

Now that we've discovered some of the great VR games that our potential users are playing and dug deep into how VR helps to make them unique, let's look at how VR can really make the experience that lets *Server 17* shine. This is where we move from the Discovery and Empathy phases of our design process into the Ideate phase. Ideate is where the magic happens and where ideas are brainstormed and transformed into something more. For our user (first-time VR user, sci-fi fan, and nostalgic), we need to take into account that their status as first time users will mean that a basic locomotion scheme is important. We also want to make sure that the gameplay is intuitive and easy to learn. Current VR controllers are capable of several button-based functions, but we'll want to keep our control scheme simple to lower the learning curve and make our game accessible. Lastly, we want to make our environment simple yet really embrace the cyberpunk and future aesthetic.

With these things in mind, let's design. To keep locomotion easy and minimize VR sickness, we can use teleportation while keeping the gameplay area small. This will have the added benefit of playing into our cyberpunk background and the fact that the game level is meant to take place in a form of VR itself. We'll have the player press buttons and manipulate objects using some avatar hands. This allows us to make the gameplay as natural as possible, as well as making it easy to grasp quickly (pun intended). Gameplay will be centered around hacking a corporate server, reimagined as a techy-looking puzzle box in the center of the room that the player will have to solve by grasping parts to push and slide. We also want to provide the player with some special tools to speed the process up. These tools will be provided at different tool stations spread around the virtual room that represents the inside of the player's computer. Finally, to represent the danger of being discovered, the player will have to complete the puzzle box within a certain time frame. Here is a rough idea of the level:

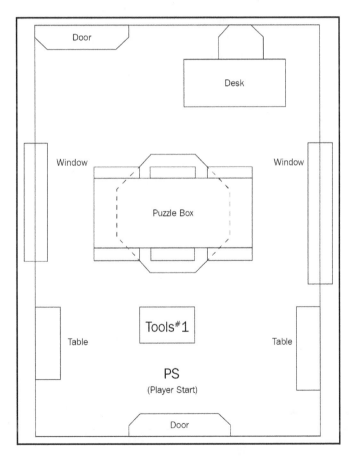

Level map with design markings

Now, your instinct might be next to decide on the art style or to start making static meshes and shaders. Resist that urge! Despite the fact that the design sounds fun on paper, we don't know whether all of the features will work as intended or whether they're even as fun as we think they'll be. To test our assumptions, we need to move to the prototype stage of our design process and build a quick functional mock up and have our user test it to gain feedback. That way, we don't waste time or resources on game elements we might not use.

We'll start by implementing the hands.

Adding the hand functionality

We want the player's experience with their in-game representation to be as smooth and as seamless as possible. To that end, the hand solution we implement needs to be able to do a few different things. First, the player needs to be able to see the hands. Second, the player needs to be able to know which objects can be interacted with and which ones might simply be there as scenery. Third, the player needs to be able to grab, pick up, and potentially throw objects that we want them to interact with. Fourth, we need the player to be able to press buttons inside the level to utilize the tools found at the different tool stations and to solve the puzzle cube.

The first step in following our design is to add the hand models to our `Server17PlayerPawn` to give our player a representation of themselves in the game. To do this, we'll add the standard hands provided for us by Epic Games to our pawn:

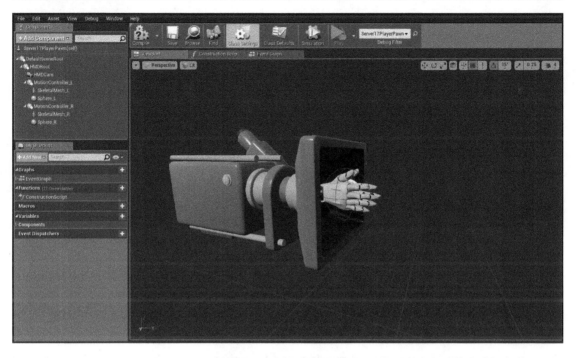

Hands added in the Class Blueprint screen

Here's how we add the hands:

1. To have the hand meshes read the position of the player's motion controls, we'll start by adding a skeletal mesh component that's attached to the **MotionController_L** component in our pawn. Click on the **MotionController_L** component, and then click the **Add Component** button at the top of the **Components** panel. Select the **Skeletal Mesh** option and name the new component SkeletalMesh_L.

2. In the **Details** panel, find the **Skeletal Mesh** drop-down menu and select the **MannequinHand_Right**. This will add the hand to the end of the player's motion controller.

3. Since the hand is meant to be a right hand, we need to change a few settings to make it work correctly as a left hand. Find the **Transform** portion of the **Details** panel and change the **X** field of the **Location** property to **-10**. This will align the mesh more with where the player's physical hand is on the controller and will feel more natural.

4. Move down to the **Rotation** property and change the **X** value to **90** degrees. This rotates the hand to a more natural position.

5. Move down one more property to the **Scale** property, and change the **Z** value to **-1**. This will flip the orientation of the hand to truly represent a left hand.

6. With the left hand complete, repeat steps one through four to create the right hand and name it `MotionController_R`.

If we test now, we can see that the player pawn now has hands! Wave them in the air like you just don't care. However, they don't really do much other than look plastic, yet well manicured. Let's start to give them some functionality with the edition of some collision shapes so we can record when they overlap with an object. Let's start with the left hand:

1. Select the **MotionController_L** component and navigate to the **Add Component** menu. Find the **Sphere Collision** component under the **Collision** section of the drop-down menu and select it. Name it `Sphere_L`.

2. In the **Details** panel, change the sphere radius to **10**. This will define the area in which objects are considered overlapping with the player's hands.

3. Repeat steps one and two to create a collision sphere for the right hand and name it `Sphere_R`.

Our hands are now set up to record overlap events so that we can manipulate objects in our game world. At this point, there are several actions we want these objects to perform. We want them to be able to detect when they're being looked at and when they're not. We also need them to know when we've performed some kind of action on them, an activated and a deactivated state. For this, we'll use something called a **Blueprint Interface**. A Blueprint Interface can be defined as a collection of one or more functions that can be assigned to objects that need to share data and functionality. It allows us to create a number of functions that each object that uses the interface can then define in a unique manner. In our game, we'll create an interface that contains all the functions that control how the hands manipulate gameplay objects.

 Tribe XR makes extensive use of Blueprint Interfaces to facilitate the creation and communication of its different user interfaces, since many of them share common elements. From the interface elements used to display music track information to the **Options** screen, they all have in common that they're 2D interfaces projected on to 3D planes. As we'll see from the following screenshot, creating a Blueprint Interface of common functions ahead of time can facilitate the creation of these menus:

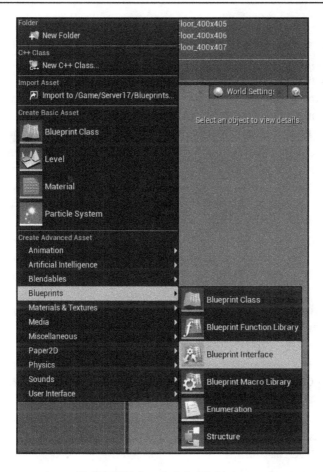

The Blueprint Interface option in the right-click menu

Start by creating a new **Blueprint Interface**:

1. Make sure we're in our `Sever17\Blueprints` folder. Right-click in the **Content Broswer** and navigate to the **Create Advanced Asset** section of the menu. Find the **Blueprints** option and select **Blueprint Interface**. Name it `ObjectInteractionInterface`.

2. Double-click `ObjectInteractionInterface` to open it.

3. We'll need to create several functions here. Over on the right-hand side of the screen in the **Functions** section of the **My Blueprints** panel, click the plus (+) button to create a new function. Name it `TraceHitObject`. This will fire whenever our object is hit by a line trace from either the motion controller or the HMD, signifying that we're looking at it or interacting with it in some way.

4. With our new function selected, look at the **Details** panel. This panel allows us to add input and output to our function to handle our data. Let's add an input named `Hit` and use the type **Hit Result**. Passing the hit data to the object allows us to access important information later.

5. To finish the function, we need to add a Boolean output named **Return**. Unreal Engine reads a function without an output as an **Event**, which isn't what we want. To avoid this, we use a dummy Boolean variable to complete the function.

6. The next function we need to create will be able to read when a trace leaves the object, giving us additional options for functionality. Head back to the **Functions** section of the `MyBlueprint` panel and create another function. Name it `TraceLeaveObject`. Create an input variable called `Hit` of the **Hit Result** type. Finish the function by creating a Boolean output and name it `Return`.

7. Now that the object can tell whether it's being looked at, let's take that functionality to the next level. It would be useful to have the object know what part of it's being looked at. We can do this by detecting the trace at the component level. Create a new function and name it `TraceHitComponent`. Just like our other functions, we need to create an input called `Hit` of the **Hit Result** type and an output called `Return` of the **Boolean** type.

8. To be able to read what component is being hit, we need to also add another input. Create a second input named `Component` and make it be of the type **Primitive Component**. This way, we can pass in what specific component is being hit.

9. Let's finish this functionality. Create another function and name it `TraceLeaveComponent`. This should have the same inputs and outputs as the `TraceHitComponent`.

10. Just a few more functions and we'll be finished! Let's create a function that can be called every frame to track the potential movement of an object. Create another function and name it `TraceMove`. This should have an input named `Hit` of the **Hit Result** type, and an output named `Return` of the **Boolean** type.

11. `TraceMove` needs one more change to make it function correctly. Since this is a function designed to be called every frame, performance is definitely a concern. To optimize this function, we'll check two options. First, under the `Hit` input, click the little arrow next to the name of the variable and click the checkbox to make the function **Pass-by-Reference**. Passing by reference allows the `Hit` variable to be passed on by name without passing the value. Because we're selecting to pass the variable in this manner, we need to select the **Const** option in the **Graph** section of the **Details** panel. If you can't see the option, click the down arrow at the bottom of the section to expose the checkbox.

12. Finally, let's create one more bit of functionality. We want to be able to activate and deactivate some kind of effect on an object. This covers a variety of potential scenarios, such as being able to turn a flashlight you picked up on and off. To create this effect, we need two more functions. First, create a new function and name it `TraceActivateDown`.

13. `TraceActivateDown` will signify when a button has been pressed to activate the object. It needs two inputs. The first is named `Hit` and has a **Hit Result** type (so that a lot of great information is packed into a hit result). The second is named `Instigator` and is of the **Pawn** type. This way, we can pass in the **Pawn** that activated the object. Finish by creating an output named `Return` of the **Boolean** type.

14. If `TraceActivateDown` represents a button press, then we need our final function for our interface to represent the release of that button. Create one final function named `TraceActivateUp`. This should have the same inputs and outputs as `TraceActivateDown`.

With everything completed, your interface should look something like this:

The My Blueprint section of ObjectInteractionInterface

`ObjectInteractionInterface` now encapsulates many of the functions we would want an object to be able to perform. However, many of them depend on being the target of a line trace to be able to operate. A **line trace** is a function that can be called that will draw a line from one point to another and report anything that's hit by the line. Using that hit data, we can do all kinds of things! For instance, we can find the distance from the player to the object. We can act on the object to change color, emit sound, or other behaviors. We can even cause the object to delete itself if we wanted to. In shooter games, this is how direct-damage weapons, such as lasers, sniper rifles, or other weapons that don't really have a projectile, work. Since our line trace will be checking where our player is looking and will likely be used to figure out where they can teleport, we'll use a parabola, or curved line, rather than a straight line for our trace. To do this, we'll create a custom component that can be added to our HMD or motion controller that projects the line trace:

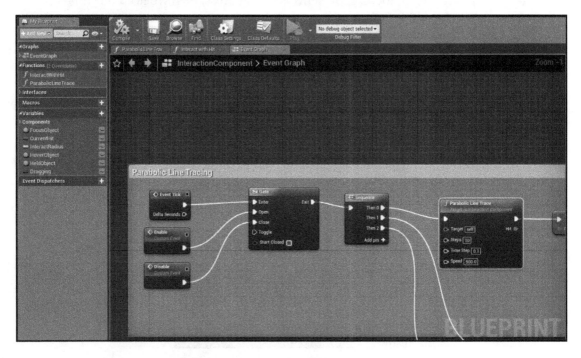

Created Interaction Component

We need to create a custom **Scene Component** that can be added to our custom pawn:

1. In the **Content Browser**, right-click in the `Server17\Blueprints` folder and click the **Blueprint Class** option. In the bottom section of the **Pick Parent Class** window, search for **Scene Component** using the search box. Click it and then click the **Select** button. Name this new component `InteractionComponent`.

2. This new component is going to handle our line trace and any data that it collects. It'll then distribute the hit data through our interface to all of our interaction functions. Start by creating a new function by clicking the +**Function** button that's part of the **My Blueprints** panel. Name this new function `ParabolicLineTrace`.

3. We calculate the parabolic curve by taking the direction the interaction component is facing and calculate the projected curve based on a fixed point in time and a speed value. The formula is $z = (t * v_z) - (0.5 * g * t^2)$, where z is the projected end of the arc in the z axis, v is the velocity, g is gravity, and t is time. The distance the arc will cover is estimated by $y = t * v_y$ where y is the end of the arc in the y axis. To have our function calculate our arc, it'll need three inputs. The first is named `Steps` and has a type of **Integer**. The second is named `TimeStep`, which is a **Float** value. Last, we have `Speed` of the **Float** type.

If you don't understand the math, don't worry! The arc it creates is perfect for estimating the final location of our future teleport. Once complete, Unreal Engine 4 will be able to visually represent our line trace to us, and it'll make sense.

4. Double-click on our new function to open it. `ParabolicLineTrace` needs six local variables to work. Find the **Local Variables** section at the bottom of the **My Blueprints** panel. Click the +**Local Variable** button and create a new variable named **Init Loc** of the type **Vector**. Next, create one named **Prev Loc**, also of the type **Vector**. These will store the initial locations for our curve calculation.

5. Create another local variable named `Velocity` of the type **Vector**. This is our speed value.

6. Now we need two local variables to handle our time calculation. Create two new local variables named `InTimeStep` of the type **Float** and **In Steps** of the type **Integer**.

7. This is the last one! We need one more local variable to hold the hit data from the line trace. Create one final local variable named `TempHit` and make sure its type is set to **Hit Result**:

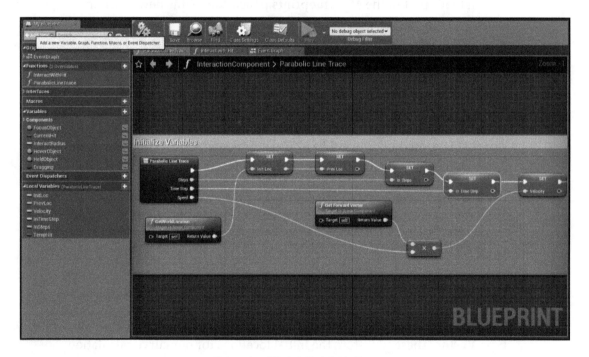

Setting up the variables in the Parabolic Line Trace

With all of our variables finally set up, we can move on to creating our curve calculation.

8. The first step in our function is to store our location data. From your **Local Variables** section, drag in a copy of your `InitLoc` variable and choose **Set**. Do the same for your `PrevLoc` variable. Connect the execute output of the beginning of the function to the input on **Init Loc**. Connect the execute output on **Init Loc** to the input on **Prev Loc**.

9. Now we need to fill them with data. We need to start by knowing the location of the interaction component within the game world. Right-click in the blueprint window or use the Palette to grab a **GetWorldLocation** node. Connect the output of our new node into the **Init Loc** vector input, and then connect the vector output on **Init Loc** to the vector input on **Prev Loc**.

10. Go back to the **Local Variables** section in **My Blueprint** and grab the **In Steps** and the `InTimeStep` variables, and choose **Set** for both of them. Connect the execute output of our **Prev Loc** node to the execute input on the **In Steps** node. Then, connect the execute output of **In Steps** to the input on **In Time Step**.

11. To finish this section, we need to connect **In Steps** and **In Time Step** to their appropriate data input. Take the `Steps` input from our function and connect that to the integer input on **In Steps**. Finally, take the **TimeStep** input from the function and plug that into the float input on **In Time Step**.

12. There's one last bit of data to initialize before we calculate the curve. To get the velocity we'll use for the calculation, we'll need to determine the forward vector of our interaction component and multiply that by the `Speed` variable we take as an input into our function. Head back to the **Local Variables** portion of the screen and drag in a copy of the `Velocity` variable. Choose **Set** from the menu. Connect the execute output from our **In Time Step** node and plug it into our new **Velocity** node.

13. Right-click in the blueprint and use the menu to find the **Get Forward Vector** node where the target is a **Scene Component**. Drag a line off the **Return Value** of the node and drop it to bring up the search menu and search for the `Vector *` `Float` node. The vector input will be the **Return Value** of the **Get Forward Vector**, and the float value will be the **Speed** input from the start of our function. The resulting value will become the input for the vector on the **Set Velocity** node:

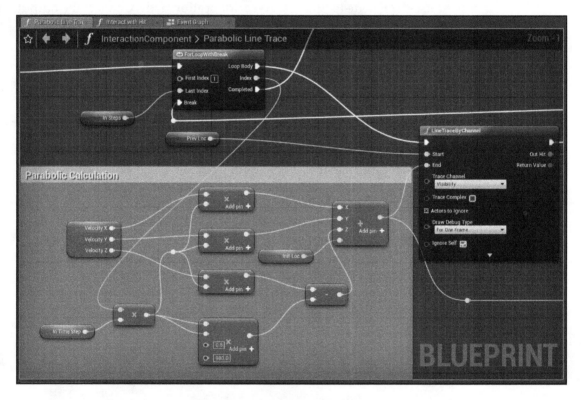

Calculating a parabolic line trace in blueprints

14. With all of our variables straightened out, it's time for the fun part! Start the calculation by creating a **ForLoopWithBreak** node. Connect the execute output from our set **Velocity** to the execute input on **ForLoopWithBreak**. Drag in a copy of our local variable **In Steps** and plug that into the **Last Index** input on **ForLoopWithBreak**. Lastly, set the **First Index** integer to **1**.

15. Next, create a **Line Trace By Channel** node. This node will do all of the heavy lifting and create the actual line trace. Plug the **Loop Body** output from the **ForLoopWithBreak** into the execute input on our new line trace. On the line trace node, change the **Draw Debug Type** to **For One Frame**. This will help us to visualize the parabolic arc. We can always turn it off later. Now grab a copy of the `PrevLoc` variable and plug that into the `Start` input on the line trace.

16. Bring on the math! Let's start by getting a copy of the `Velocity` local variable. Right-click on the output of the variable and choose the **Split Struct Pin** option. This displays all the values that make up our velocity vector.

17. Now create three copies of the `Float * Float` node. We're going to plug the X, Y, and Z values we just exposed on the **Velocity** node into the top input on each of the multiplication nodes.

18. Create a copy of the `InTimeStep` local variable and an `Integer * Float` node. Plug the output of the variable into the float input on the multiplication node. The input for the integer section of the node comes from the `Index` output of the **ForLoopWithBreak** node. The output from this bit of math will be used by many nodes.

19. Take the output and plug it into the second float input on the multiplication nodes we created earlier in *step 17*.

Don't forget, you can create reroute nodes to help clean your code! Right-click in the **Blueprint** as if you're creating a new node and find the **Reroute** node down toward the bottom of the menu.

20. It's time to compensate for gravity in our calculation. Create a `Float * Float` node and place it near the multiplication node created in *step 18*. On the newly created node, there's a button labeled **+ Add Pin**. Let's click that twice to create two more input pins. Plug the output of the multiplication node from *step 18* into the first two input values of our new node (this represents time being squared in our equation). In the third input, change the value to 0.5. In the final input, change the value to 980.

21. We've almost finished the math. Create a `Float - Float` node and plug the output of the multiplication node we use with the Z value from our `Velocity` variable into the first input and the output of the multiplication node we created in *step 20* into the second input.

22. Finally, create one final math node, `Vector + Vector`, and right-click on the first `Vector` input pin. Select **Split Struct Pin** from the menu. The *X* value will be the output of the **X Velocity** multiplication node. The *Y* will be the output of the **Y Velocity** multiplication node. The *Z* value will be the output of the `Float - Float` we created in the last step. All of that will be added to the value of **Init Loc**. Create a copy of the variable and plug into the last input. The output of this node will become the **End** vector input on our line trace node.

There's one last section regarding this function. With our **Line Trace by Channel** node getting all of the information it needs, we need to set up the output values to store the information that we receive from the trace. We'll do this by updating the location we've stored in our **Prev Loc** node and saving the hit result information into the **TempHit** node:

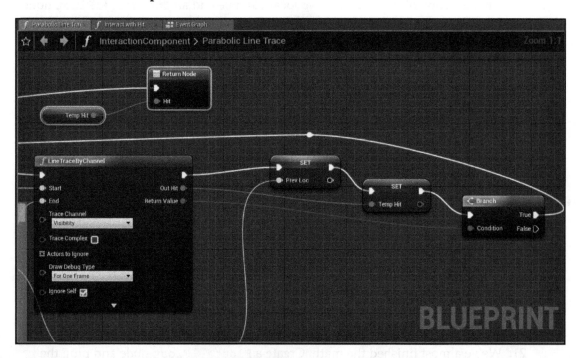

Completing the line trace

Let's wrap this thing up!

23. Create a **SET** node for our `PrevLoc` variable and connect the execute output from the line trace to its execute input. To update the vector input, drag a connection from the `Vector + Vector` node we created in *step 22* and plug it into the input.

24. Next, create a **Set** node for the **Temp Hit** local variable and connect the execute output from our set **Prev Loc** node to the execute input. Connect the **Out Hit** output from the line trace into the input.

25. To make sure that we aren't making any unnecessary hit calculations when no hit is found, let's add a **Branch** node. Add a **Branch** node and connect the execute output from the set **TempHit** node to it. Pass the **Return Value** output from the line trace into the **Condition** input.

26. Bring the execute output from this node all of the way back to the **ForLoopWithBreak** node and plug it into the **Break** input.

27. Finish this by connecting the complete execute output to the input on the function's **Return** node. Create a copy of **TempHit** and pass that into the function's output.

Now that the **Parabolic Line Trace** function is finally complete (wow! There's a lot going on there), it's time to do something with the hit information that it collects. The **Interact With Hit** function will take the hit data from the line trace and pass it to our functions we created in the **Object Interaction Interface**:

The variables for the InteractWithHit function

Let's start by creating some variables:

1. In the **My Blueprints** panel, find the **Variables** section and click the **+Variable** button. The first one we'll create will be named the `FocusComponent`. Set the **Variable Type** to **Primitive Component**. This will allow us to work with the individual components of an object as well as the object itself. Next, create a new variable named `FocusObject` and set the type to `Actor`. This will store the current object being hit. Finally, create a variable named `CurrentHit` and make its type `Hit Result` to store the hit information we collected from the line trace. Once we've created all three variables, click on each one and mark them **Private** in the **Details** panel.

2. It's time to create our second function. In the **Functions** section of **My Blueprint**, click the **+Function** button and name the new function `InteractWithHit`. The new function needs to have the ability to pass hit data into it. Click on the function, and in the **Details** panel create a new input named `Hit` of the type **Hit Result**.

3. Now we need to set up three **Local Variables** inside our new function. Double-click the `InteractWithHit` function and head to the **Local Variables** section. Click the **+Local Variable** button and name the new variable `InHitComponent` of the type **Primitive Component**. Create a second local variable and name it **In Hit** of the type **Hit Result**. Lastly, create a third local variable and name it **In Hit Actor**, and make it of the type **Actor**.

4. The initial setup is complete! With our variables created, we can now start initializing them with data. Starting at the function node, grab a copy of our **In Hit** local variable, and choose **Set** from the resulting menu. Connect the execute output from the function node to the input on the set **In Hit** node. We also want to pass the **Hit** data coming from outside of the function, so we'll connect the **Hit** pin on the function node to the input on the set **In Hit** node:

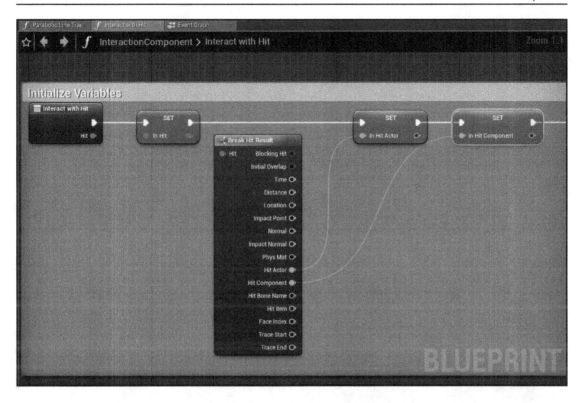

Taking in the hit data and storing it in our variables

5. Next, we're going to break the hit down and pass the **Hit Actor** and the **Hit Component** data to our local variables so that we can work with them. Right-click in the blueprint and create a **Break Hit Result** node. Connect the variable output of the **Set In Hit** node to the input on our new node. This will break the hit information down into its parts. Next, bring in a copy of our **In Hit Actor** and the InHitComponent variables, and choose **Set** from the menu. With the two setters created, connect them in the order you see in the previous screenshot. Then, connect the **Hit Actor** output from **Break Hit Result** to the input on the set **In Hit Actor** node. Be sure to do the same for **Hit Component** and the InHitComponent node.

6. Much of what we're doing here is checking the data to see whether what we're looking at can be interacted with and then passing that information through the interface we created earlier. We also need to be able to clear our variables if we're no longer looking at something that has interaction. The first step in this process is to check to see whether the object we're looking at (stored in **Focus Object**) is equal to the one we're currently looking at, and for that we need a `Branch` node. Create a new `Branch` node and connect its execute input to the output from the **Set** `InHitComponent`. Now we need the two variables we want to compare. Get a copy of our **Focus Object** variable and our **In Hit Actor** local variable. Drag a connection off **FocusObject** and drop it to open the search menu. Look for the **Equal** (Object) node. This will compare two objects passed into it and return a Boolean showing whether they match. Connect the **In Hit Actor** to the second input and run the Boolean output into the input pin on the **Branch**:

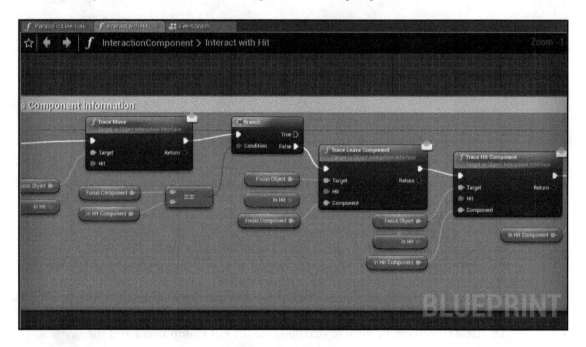

Passing the data through our interface

7. With our **Branch** ready, it's time to pass the information. From the `True` output, drag a connection off and drop it to search for our **Trace Move** (message) function that we created earlier in the **Object Interaction Interface**. Get a copy of the **Focus Object** variable and pass that into the **Target** pin on **Trace Move**. Now get a copy of the **In Hit** variable and connect that to the `Hit` input on **Trace Move**.

8. Create another **Branch** node and connect its execution input to the output from **Trace Move**. This time, we'll be checking to see whether the **Focus Object** is equal to the `InHitComponent` and passing the new information along if it's not. To do that, we need to get the **Focus Object** and the `InHitComponent` and use our **Equal** (object) node to compare them. Take the Boolean output of that comparison and plug it into the input on the new **Branch**.

9. The next node we need is another function from our interface. Right-click and search for **Trace Leave Component** (message). Create it and connect it to the **False** output on the last **Branch**. For input, we'll need to get a copy of the **FocusObject** and pass that into **Target**, **In Hit**, and pass that into **Hit**, and the **FocusComponent** and pass that into **Component**.

10. Now that we've called leave on the current focused component, we'll call the **Trace Hit Component** and have it pass the current component we're looking at. Create a copy of the **Trace Hit Component** (message) and connect it to the **Trace Leave Component**. Pass **FocusObject** into **Target**, **In Hit** into **Hit**, and `InHitComponent` into **Component**.

11. There is one final step in this branch of the process. We need to set the **FocusComponent** to our new the `InHitComponent`. Create a **Set** node for the **FocusComponent**, and get a copy of the `InHitComponent`. Connect the execute output from the **Trace Hit Component** to set the **FocusComponent** and pass the `InHitComponent` into the variable input pin.

12. The branch we created was all about passing component data if the **Focus Object** and the **In Hit** object we're looking at are the same, but what if they're different? If they are, we need to clear the hit data and pass the new hit information through the interface. Go back to the **Branch** we created way back in *step 6*. Drag a connection from the `False` output and drop it. Search for the **Trace Leave Object** function and create the node. The **Trace Leave Object** has two input values. Into the **Target** input, we'll pass the object we're currently storing in the **FocusObject**. For the `Hit` input, get the current value of **In Hit** and connect it to the input pin:

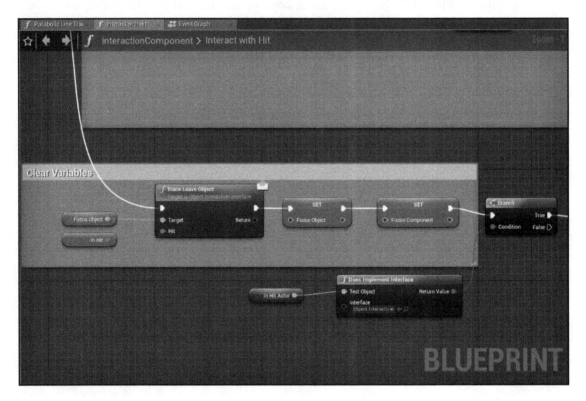

Clearing the variables

13. Since we're leaving the object and turning our focus elsewhere, we'll need to clear the values stored in the **FocusObject** and the **FocusComponent**. Create a **Set** version of each of the variables. Connect the new set **FocusObject** node to the execute output from **Trace Leave Object**. Connect the new set **FocusComponent** node to the set **FocusObject** node. We're leaving both of their input values empty to clear their values.

14. Before we pass the new hit data forward, there's still one more check we need to do. We only want to pass on the hit information if the object we're looking at makes use of the Object Interaction Interface, since anything else wouldn't matter to us. It's our way as designers of creating objects that are interactable and others that are only meant to be scenery. To do this, we'll use another **Branch** node. Connect the input for the new branch to the execution output from the set **FocusComponent**. To check to see whether the object we're looking at uses the interface, we need to use the **Does Implement Interface** function. This function takes in an **Actor** and checks to see whether it has a specific interface attached to it, then returns a Boolean value—perfect for using with the **Branch** node. Create a copy of the **Does Implement Interface**. Pass in the value of the **In Hit Actor** as the **Test Object** and then click the drop-down menu under **Interface**. Use the search box at the top of the menu to find our **Object Interaction Interface**. With that set, plug the **Return** value from the node into the Condition input on our **Branch**. Our check is all set up:

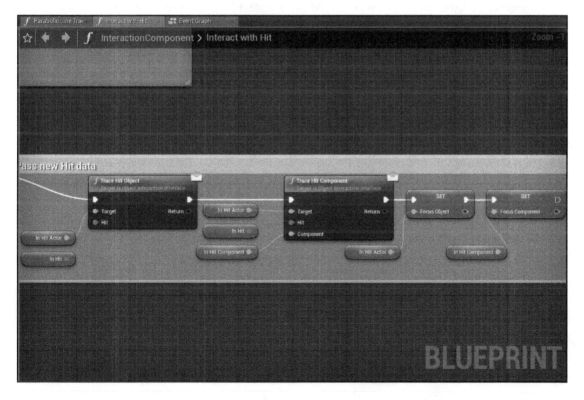

Passing in the new hit data

15. Now all that's left is to pass on is the new hit data. Right-click in the blueprint and search for **Trace Hit Object** (message). Connect it to the **True** output from the **Branch** and pass the **In Hit Actor** into the **Target** input and the **In Hit** into the **Hit** input.

16. Next, create a copy of the **Trace Hit Component** (message) function. Pass the **In Hit Actor** into the **Target** input, **In Hit** into the **Hit** input, and the **InHitComponent** into the **Component** input.

17. In the final step for this branch, we'll need to update the values store in the **FocusObject** and the **FocusComponent** with the values from the **In Hit Actor** and the `InHitComponent`. Create a set **FocusObject** node and connect it to the execute output of the **Trace Hit Component** function. Pass the value of the **In Hit Actor** into the variable input. Lastly, connect the set **FocusComponent** execute input to the execute output from set the `FocusActor` and pass in the value from the `InHitComponent`. We've now completely finished using this function!

It's taken quite a bit of programming to get here, hasn't it? However, we have made a huge amount of progress in building our hand interactions. Our **Interaction Component** now has the ability to do a parabolic line trace to find objects and safe locations to teleport. It can now pass information through the Object Interaction Interface we created to allow our interactable objects to work with the hands, to create gameplay. It's now time to bring that all together in the Event Graph to implement all of the functionality we've created. For this, we'll use the **Event Tick** node:

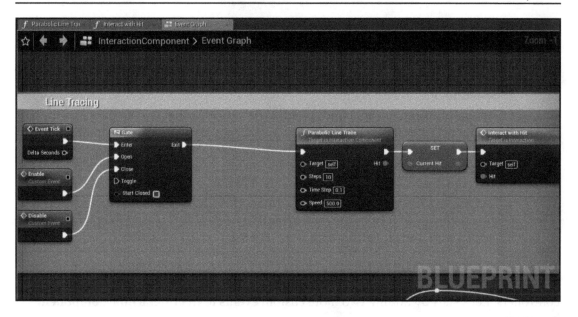

Triggering the Parabolic Line Trace

Start by creating a couple of **Custom Events**:

1. We'll need two custom events to represent the on and off states that we want the **Interaction Component** to have. The **Custom Events** will be called by elements outside this blueprint to trigger interaction using button presses on the player's motion controllers. Right-click near the **Event Tick** node and find the **Add Event** section of the menu. Open it and select the **Add Custom Event** option. Name this new event `Enable`. Repeat the process to create a second custom event and name it `Disable`.

2. Next, we'll use a **Gate** node to only allow the player to interact with objects when they've enabled the interaction component with a button. A **Gate** is a flow-control node that opens and shuts to allow data through only when the programmer allows it. Right-click in the blueprint and search for the **Gate** node. We'll connect the **Event Tick** output to the **Enter** input on the **Gate**. To control the flow of data, we'll connect the **Execution** output from our **Enable** custom event to the **Open** input and the execution output from the **Disable** custom event to the **Close** input.

3. Now we'll add in our **Parabolic Line Trace** function. Grab a copy of it from the **My Blueprints** panel and drag it into the blueprint. Connect the execute output from the **Gate** to the execution input on the function. To make sure our parabola functions correctly, set the number of **Steps** to 10, the **Time Step** to 0.1, and the **Speed** to 500.

4. The output from our line trace needs to be stored so that we can pass it to the **Interact With Hit** function. Luckily, we already created a variable to hold it. Create a copy of our CurrentHit hit variable by dragging it in from the **My Blueprint** panel and select **Set** from the menu. Connect it to the execute output from the line trace function and pass the **Hit** output from the line trace into it.

5. End the sequence by bringing in the **Interact With Hit** function and connecting the execute output from the set **CurrentHit** node to it. Connect the variable output from the set **CurrentHit** as the **Hit** input on the function.

There's one final piece to this interaction puzzle. We need to add the interaction component to Server17PlayerPawn and map the functionality to buttons on the player's motion controllers. Let's start by adding two more custom events to the **Interaction Component** blueprint:

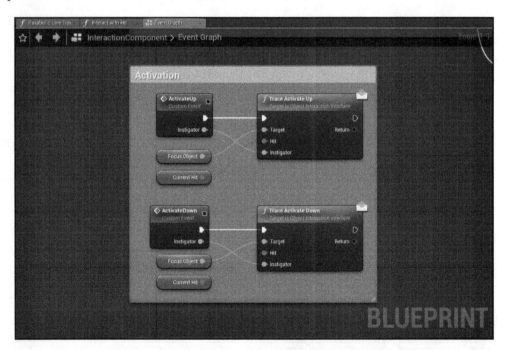

Activation section of the Interaction Blueprint

Every button has two states: an up and a down. We'll define these states by creating two Custom Events:

1. Right-click in a new section of the blueprint, find the **Add Event** section of the menu, and open it and choose **Add Custom Event**. Name the first one `ActivateUp`. Create a second custom event and name it `ActivateDown`. Both events need to have a single input. Click on each of the custom events and click the + button in the **Inputs** section of the **Details** panel. Name the input `Instigator` and make its type **Pawn**.

2. Drag a connection off **ActivateUp** and search for **Trace Activate Up** (message). We created this function as part of our interface. Connect its execution to the **ActivateUp** event and connect the **Instigator** output from the event to the **Instigator** input on the function.

3. **Trace Activate Up** still needs two more input values to work correctly. Get a copy of the `FocusObject` variable and connect that to the **Target** input. Lastly, get a copy of the `CurrentHit` variable and connect that to the `Hit` input on the function.

4. We're going to repeat this process for `ActivateDown`—only, this time, we'll connect the **Trace Activate Down** (message) function from our interface.

It's time to finish the setup in the player pawn:

Components setup in the player pawn

Start by adding a copy of the **Interaction Component** to each of the hands:

1. In the **Content Browser**, find the `Server17PlayerPawn` and double-click to open it.
2. In the **Viewport** tab, head over to the **Components** panel and click the **Add Component** button. Use the search box to find our **Interaction Component** that we created. It'll be under the heading **Custom**. Click on it and name the new component `InteractionComponent_L`.
3. Drag and drop the new component on to the **MotionController_L** component.
4. Repeat *step 2* and *step 3* to create a second interaction component that's a child of the right motion controller. Name this one `InteractionComponent_R`.
5. Now we can tie our new interaction components to buttons on the controllers. This will give the player the power to finally interact with the world! Click on the **Event Graph** tab. In an empty section of the graph, right-click and search for the **MotionController (L) Trigger** event. Repeat the process to create a node for the **MotionController (R) Trigger** event:

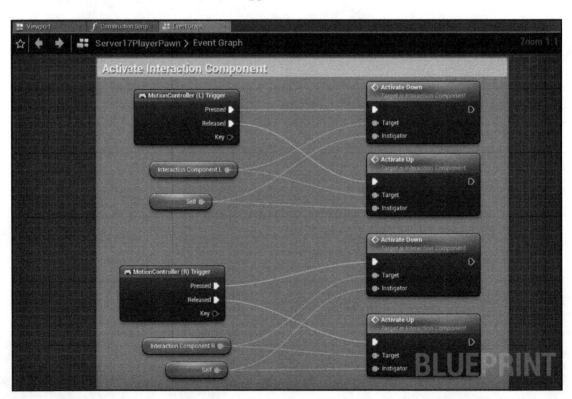

Mapping actions to our motion controllers in the player pawn

6. For each of our button events, we need to create two references to our custom events that we created back in the interaction component blueprint. Start by grabbing a reference to the left interaction component from the **My Blueprints** panel. Position it near the **MotionController (L) Trigger** event. Drag a line off it and drop it. Use the search box to find our **Activate Down** function. Connect it to the **Pressed execute** output on the left trigger event. Next, drag a connection off the **Instigator** input pin on the **Activate Down** function and drop it to bring up the search menu. Search for a reference to the Self variable. In this case, the player is the instigator of the activation.

7. Repeat the process for the **MotionController (R) Trigger** event by using a reference to the right interaction component.

I chose to use the left and right triggers for interactions for a couple different reasons. First, it's a button that's natural for a first-time user to press to activate something or to make something happen. It's intuitive. Second, the button event exists with the Oculus Touch controllers and Vive motion controllers, so I wouldn't have to change anything to go between hardware. Later, we'll create a pickup interaction, and I will use the grip buttons for the same reasons.

In this first section of programming, we set up the hand static meshes and programmed the ObjectInteractionInterface, a collection of functions that can be utilized by the object we want the player to be able to interact with. This blueprint interface connects to our **Interfaction Component**, a custom **Scene Component** that has the ability to utilize a parabolic line trace function to find interactive objects. Finally, we mapped our **Activate** functionality to buttons on the **Motion Controller** as part of **Player Pawn** blueprint. In the next section, we'll build on to this new functionality to create a teleport mechanic.

Building the teleportation

Now that the code for line tracing and interaction has been implemented, we can turn our attention to the teleport system itself. The goal of using teleportation in *Server 17* is to give our player an intuitive method of moving around our environment. Though teleportation is often seen as immersion breaking, I feel that the cyberspace environment in our game supports the idea of the player character being able to teleport around the space. To get started, let's first think about the parts of a VR teleport system:

- **Visuals**: Players need to be able to visualize where they'll be moving to when they click the button. This can be done by projecting a line or an arc to where they'll land (we've done this through the debug option on our line trace that we set earlier). We should also have a visual on the surface they'll land on, to further highlight their landing point. Lastly, we might think about a particle effect and/or a sound effect to help enhance the player experience.
- **Teleport code**: This would be the actual functionality that's built within the blueprint. The code will need to handle the displaying of the visual elements, as well as the teleport itself. It would also be nice to build in some kinds of controls for us as designers to restrict the player to certain areas so that they can't teleport outside the area we've built for them or see things they aren't supposed to.

Contrary to how we would normally start building a feature such as this (functionality, then art), here we'll start with a bit of the visual components. In this case, we need some visuals to be able to turn on and off to make sure our code is working. Building this system will also be an excellent test of how our interface and line trace code is working. Let's start with a visual on the ground for teleporting:

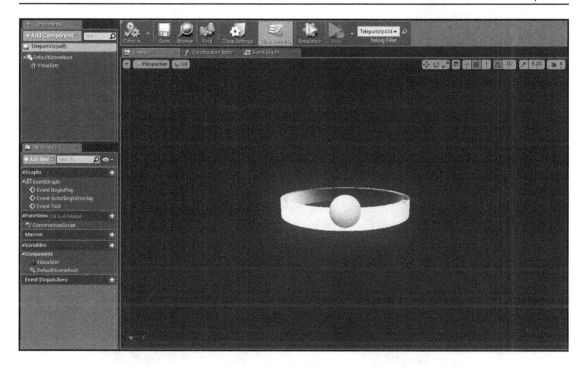

TeleportViz viewport

We start by creating a new actor blueprint:

1. Right-click in the `Server17\Blueprints` folder of the **Content Browser** and select the **Blueprint Class** option from the **Create Basic Asset** section of the menu. Choose **Actor** from the **Pick Parent Class** menu and name this new blueprint **TeleportViz**. Double-click the blueprint to open it.

2. In the **Viewport** tab, head over to the **Components** panel and click the **Add Component** button. Choose **Static Mesh** from the menu. This should create a new static mesh component that's a child of the **Default Scene Root**.

3. Click on it and search for the **Static Mesh** section of the **Details** panel. There's an option called **Static Mesh** where we can set the shape we want to use. Click the drop-down menu and search for **SM_FatCylinder**, though you may use any shape you like. Name the piece `Visualizer`.

4. The static mesh looks a bit plain. Let's spruce it up a bit with a custom **Material** to make it glow a bit and stand out. This will also serve as a great test for a potential art style for the overall environment of the game. In the **Content Browser**, navigate to the `Server17` folder, right-click in the **Content Browser** window, and create a **New Folder**. Name it `Materials`. Double-click the new folder and right-click in it to create a new **Material**. Name this material `M_TeleportViz`. Double-click the new material to open it:

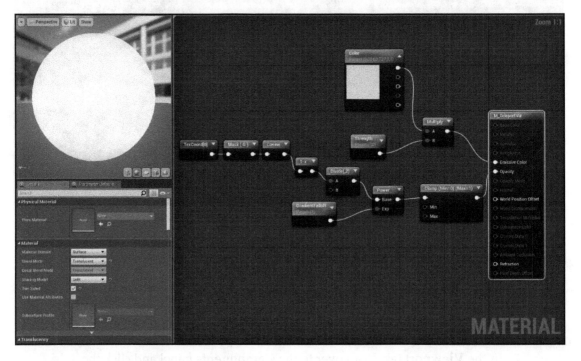

TeleportViz Material

5. When we open the material, we're greeted with one large **Result Node** to get us started. Click on it, and let's tweak a few of the settings in the **Details** panel. Find the option labeled **Blend Mode**. We want our new material to feel high-tech, so let's change the mode to **Translucent** to give it a little bit of that feel. Next, find the **Shading Model**. Since we're going to give this element an emissive glow, let's change the model to **Unlit**. Lastly, check the box to make the material **Two Sided**.

6. Now it's time to choose a color. Create a **Constant 3 Vector** by grabbing it from the **Palette** panel or holding the 3 key and clicking in the material blueprint. If you don't have the **Palette** open and would like it to be, click on the window button at the top right of your screen and choose **Palette** from the menu. Right-click on the new vector and select **Convert to Parameter** at the top of the resulting menu. Name the parameter **Color**. By making it a parameter, we're making it possible to use blueprints to change it if we needed to. This could be handy in the future.

7. Click on the **Color** node and click on the block of color in the **Details** panel to bring up the color picker. Choose any color you like and click the **Ok** button. If you would like to use the light blue color I have, set your RGB values to *R=0.84*, *G=0.74*, and *B=1.0*. Make sure you **Alpha** is set to *A=1.0*.

8. To give the material a bit of glow, let's create a **Constant** value and multiply that by our **Color**. Search for **Constant** in the **Palette** or right-click and use the search box. Right-click on the new node and select **Convert to Parameter** as we did for **Color** in *step 6*. Over in the **Details** panel, name this value **Strength** and set the default value to 10. Finally, create a **Multiply** node and connect the output of the **Color** parameter as value A and the output of **Strength** as value B. Finish by connecting the output of the multiply to the **Emissive** slot on the **Result** node.

9. To give our new **Color** a bit of a gradient effect, we'll manipulate the texture coordinates a bit. Create a **Texture Coordinate** node by either using the **Palette** or holding the *U* key and clicking in the blueprint.

10. Next, we'll need a **Component Mask**. Create a copy of the node using the **Palette** or right-click in the blueprint and use the search box. In the **Details** panel, turn off the option to use the **R** channel. Connect the output from the **Texture Coordinate** to the input on the **Component Mask**.

11. Now create a **Cosine** node. A **Cosine** will ensure that the gradient starts from both ends of the material. This will connect to the output from the **Component Mask**.

12. **Cosine** outputs a value between -1 and 1. We need the resulting value to be positive only, so we'll use a **One Minus** node. This will give us values between 0 and 2. Create the **One Minus** node and connect it to the output of the **Cosine** node.

13. To bring the value back to between 0 and 1, we can divide the answer by 2. Using the **Divide** node, connect the output of the **One Minus** node as the A value. Click on the **Divide** node and find the value for B in the **Details** panel. Change this value to 2.0.

14. Now we're going to build in some control over the distance the gradient takes to go from opaque to clear. This is called **Falloff**. Create a new **Power** node and connect the output of our **Divide** node into the **Base** input on the new node. Next, create a **Constant**. This can be done using the **Palette** or the search menu, or by holding the one key and clicking in the blueprint. Right-click on it and **Convert to Parameter**. Name the parameter `GradientFalloff` and set the **Default Value** to 3. Plug the output of this parameter into the **Exponent**, or **Exp**, input on the **Power** node.

15. To ensure the resulting value can never go above 1, we'll need to clamp the value. Create a new **Clamp** node and bring in the output from the **Power** node. Plug the output of the **Clamp** node into the **Opacity** slot on the result node.

16. Check that out! The result should be glowing and partially see-through. You can tweak the materials by adjusting the **GradientFalloff**, **Strength**, and **Color** parameters until it feels right to you. To complete the visual, head back to our **TeleportViz** class blueprint and click on the static mesh component. Using the **Details** panel, apply our new material and bask in the high-tech glow.

With the visual component sorted, we can now build the functionality. To meet our needs of a system that can control where a player can teleport, we're going to create a volume that only allows players to teleport where we place it. It'll display our visual elements when it detects a line trace and will contain our teleport code. Start by right clicking in the `Server17\Blueprints` folder of the **Content Browser** and create a new **Blueprint Class**. Choose **Actor** from the **Pick Parent Class** menu and name it `TeleportVol`:

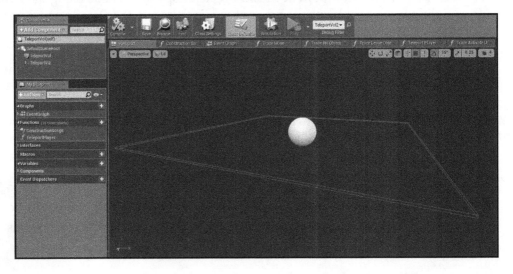

The TeleportVol component

We'll start in the **Viewport** tab:

1. **TeleportVol** has two components that make it work. The first is a box volume to detect collisions and line traces. The second is the visual elements we created earlier that we can turn on and off. Start by heading to the **Components** panel and creating a new **Box Collision**. Name the new component `TeleportVol`.

2. Click on **TeleportVol** in the **Component** panel. We want the collision box to cover a fair amount of space, but it really doesn't have to be that tall. In the **Details Panel**, find the **Box Extents** entry and change the values to *X=200, Y=200,* and *Z=1.0.*

3. Now we need to customize the collision a bit. In the **Collision** section of the **Details** panel, find the **Collision** section. Choose the **Collision Presets** drop-down menu and change it to **Custom**. Under **Trace Responses**, we want to set both options to **Block**. In the **Object Responses** section, change all of the options to **Ignore**. This will make the volume available for line traces, but nothing else.

4. With the volume customized, we can move on to the second component. In the **Components** panel, click the **Add Component** button and select **Child Actor** from the menu. This is a copy of a class blueprint that we can place inside this blueprint. We can essentially build a class blueprint out of class blueprints! Click the component and find the **Child Actor** Class option in the **Details** panel. Using the drop-down menu, set this option to **TeleportViz**. We also don't want it to be visible unless it's being hit by a line trace, so turn off the **Visible** option in the **Rendering** section of the **Details**.

5. Now we will move on to the code! We need this object to be able to react to line traces, right? Well, we wrote a whole interface for exactly that. This will be the first application of our Object Interaction Interface. To add the functions from the interface to this object, click on the **Class Defaults** that's just above the area where the **Event Graph** and **Viewport** tabs are located. This will open the default options for this class over in the **Details** panel. Find the **Interfaces** section and click the **Add** button. Search for the **Object Interaction Interface** in the menu and select it to add its functions to our teleport volume.

6. We now have access to every function we wrote in the interface. These can be found in the **Interfaces** section of the **My Blueprint** panel. Simply click the **Arrow** next to the word **Interfaces** to see them. We can even double-click on their names to open them. Open the following functions: `TraceMove`, `TraceHit`, `TraceLeaveObject`, and `TraceActivateUp`:

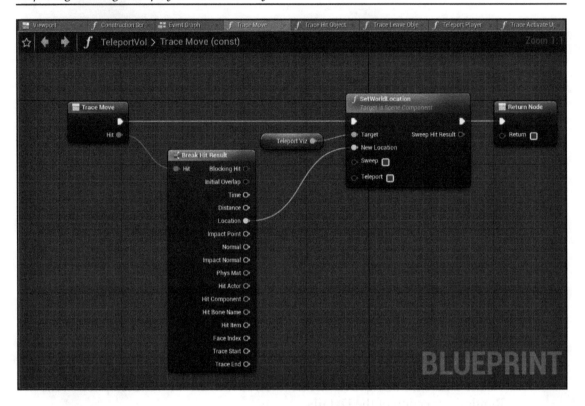

The Trace Move function

7. For **Trace Move**, we need to program what happens as a line trace moves across our object. For the teleport volume, we want the visual element we created earlier (the glowing ring, **TeleportViz**) to move to wherever our line trace is hitting. To do this, we'll use a **SetWorldLocation** node. Right-click in the blueprint and search for **Set World location**. Choose **SetWorldLocation** (**TeleportViz**) from the list. Connect the execute output of the function node to its input and the execute output to the **Return** node.

8. **SetWorldLocation** needs a **New Location** input to know where to move **TeleportViz** to, and we can find that by breaking down the **Hit** result that comes as an input into the function. Create a **Break Hit Result** node and bring in the **Hit** from the function node as the input. We can take the **Location** output from the break and use that as the **New Location** input on the **Set World Location**.

9. Next, choose the **TraceHit** function. In this function, we want to turn on the visibility of our **TeleportViz** mesh so that our player can see where they'll appear. Right-click in the blueprint and create a **Set Visibility (TeleportViz)** node. Connect it to the function node and to the **Return** node. On the node, turn on the **New Visibility** checkbox and the **propagate to children** checkbox.

10. Now, let's move on to the **TraceLeaveObject** function. This function will do something very similar to the **TraceHit** function, except we'll be turning the visibility back to off. Similar to the preceding, create a **Set Visibility (TeleportViz)** node and connect it to both the function node and the **Return** node. On the node itself, leave the box next to **New Visibility** unchecked, but do click the checkbox next to **Propagate** to **Children**:

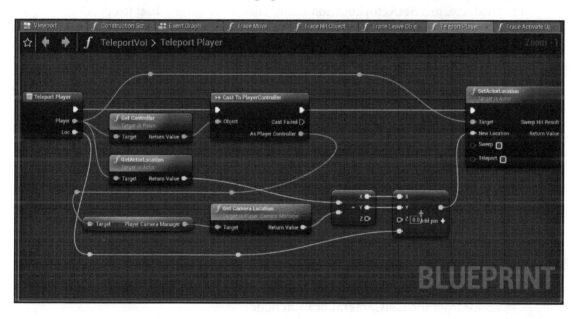

The Teleport function

11. Before we move on to the `TraceActivateUp`, we need to create a function that can handle the mechanics of the teleport. Over in the **Functions** section of the **My Blueprint** panel, click the + button and name the new function **Teleport Player**. **Teleport Player** needs to have a couple of input values to work. The first is named `Player` and will be of the type **Actor**. The second will be named `Loc` and this will be of the type **Vector**.

12. The teleport itself will require a little bit of math and will need a bit of info from our **Player Controller**. Let's start the sequence by dragging an execute line from the function node and dropping it to open the search menu. Search for the **Cast to PlayerController** node and create it. Casting allows us to pretend to be another blueprint and is just one of many ways that allow us to communicate data between blueprints.

13. Casting requires an **Object** input, a reference to the specific object we're pretending to be to access its data. To get the exact **PlayerController** we need, click and drag a line off the **Player** input on the function node and drop it. Search for the **Get Controller** node and connect its output to the input on the **Cast** to **PlayerController** node.

14. Next, create a **SetActorLocation** node. This will do the actual teleporting by moving the player to the designated vector coordinates. Connect the execution output from the cast into the execution input on **SetActorLocation**. The target input should be set to the **Player** by dragging a connection from the **Player** input on the function node to the **Target** input on **SetActorLocation**.

15. It's now time to calculate the new location! To start, we'll need to get the location of two things: the player and the player camera. To get the player's location, drag a line off the **Player** input on the function node and drop it to open the search box. Search for the **GetActorLocation** node and create one. We'll need this data in a moment.

16. Drag a line off the as **Player Controller** output from our **Cast** to **PlayerController** node and use it to search for the **Get Player Camera Manager** node. Drag off the output of that and search for the **Get Camera Location** node.

17. Here is the math part: We need to subtract the location of the player's camera from the location of the player itself to find the true location of the HMD for our teleport. For that, we'll need a **Vector - Vector** node. The top input will be the vector output from our **GetActorLocation** node. The bottom input will be the vector from the **GetCameraLocation** node.

18. We're almost there! Right-click on the output pin of our `Vector - Vector` node and split the struct pin. We only need the **X** and **Y** value for the next part of the calculation. Create a new `Vector + Vector` node and split the struct pin on the top input. Connect the **X** and **Y** output values from `Vector - Vector` into the *X* and *Y* input values on the `Vector + Vector` node. The bottom vector input comes from the **Loc** input from the function node. Drag a connection from the **Loc** input on the function node and connect it to the bottom vector input on the `Vector + Vector`.

Don't forget that you can use reroute nodes to clean up your code to make it organized and readable. Reroute nodes can be found in the search menu if you drag off a connection and drop it. They can also be created by double-clicking on the connection where you would like to create one.

19. With that, the calculation is complete! Plug the output from the `Vector + Vector` node into the **New Location** input on **SetActorLocation** to complete the sequence:

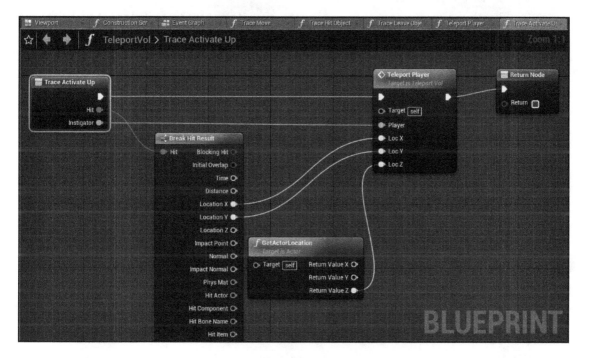

Trace Activate Up

20. The last function to program is **Trace Activate Up**, or what happens when a player releases the button of their motion controller. Click the tab we opened earlier or double-click the function name in the **Functions** section of the **My Blueprint** panel. Using our new **Teleport Player** function, we're going to move the player to the new location. Grab a copy of our **Teleport Player** function and drag it into the blueprint. Connect the **Instigator** input from the function node to the **Player** input on **Teleport Player**.

21. Calculating the exact location to teleport to just a bit more math. Drag a line off the **Hit** input on the function node and drop it to open the search menu. Create a **Break Hit Result** node and right-click on the **Location** output to split the struct.

22. Create a **Get Actor Location** node and position it near the **Break Hit** node. Right-click on the vector output and split that struct pin as well.

23. Next, right-click on the **Loc** input on the **Teleport Player** node and (you guessed it!) split the struct pin.

24. It's time to pass in the *XYZ* values! Connect the **Location X** and **Location Y** outputs from **Break Hit** to the **Loc X** and **Loc Y** inputs on **Teleport Player**. Also, connect the **Z** output from the **Get Actor Location** node to the **Loc Z** input on **Teleport Player**.

25. Finish the sequence by connecting the execute output from **Teleport Player** to the **Function Return** node.

With the teleport volume complete, we can now test our ability to teleport, as well as all of the systems that support it (parabolic line tracing and the Object Interaction Interface). Throw a few of the **TeleportVol** blueprints down in your test level and go nuts trying it out! If everything works, we can move on to building a prototype puzzle box.

The server – Building the puzzle box

With the player now having the ability to touch things and teleport around our test level, it's now time tackle the puzzle box. In *Server 17*, the puzzle box is a graphical representation of the player hacking into a remote server and stealing data. The final version may contain several puzzles to solve and dozens of steps to complete. However, for this first prototype version, we're going to design and build a simple three-step box as shown as follows:

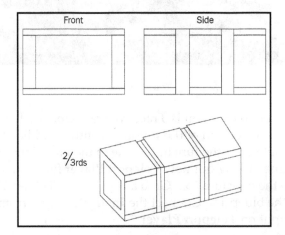

This design requires the player to find and remove a panel on the box to reveal a button that unlocks the front of the box. This panel can then be removed by grabbing it and moving it to the side revealing another switch. The final step is to then press the switch and find the removable panel to steal the data.

Building this in Unreal Engine 4 will have us creating a few things:

1. We'll need to create additional functionality for the hands that our interface currently doesn't cover, such as grabbing, dragging, and pressing.
2. We'll need an object that responds to the player's touch and can be grabbed, moved, and thrown.
3. We'll need interactive buttons that can trigger events.
4. We'll need to build the box itself using child actors and code to turn the interactive elements on and off.

When complete, we'll have an amazing test platform that can be used to prove that *Server 17* is fun and that can be tested by our target demographic. The first step in moving forward is to build a second interface to hold our button interactions:

Button Interaction Interface

It's time to create the Button Interaction Interface:

1. Head to the **Content Browser** and navigate to our `Server17\Blueprints` folder. Right-click in the browser and navigate to the **Create Advanced Asset** section of the menu. Highlight the **Blueprint Entry** and choose the **Blueprint Interface** option. Name the new interface `ButtonInteractionInterface`. Double-click the new interface to open it.

2. In this interface, we'll create nine different functions that represent the different states of the actions we're creating. The first is a function to determine what to do when we're hovering our hand over something. Find the **Functions** section of the **My Blueprint** panel and click the + button. Name the new function OnHover. OnHover will need one input named Interactor of the type **Interaction Component**. It'll also need an output named **Return** of the Boolean type to make it function properly.

3. The next function will be named EndHover and controls what happens when the player's hand leaves an object. It has the same input and output as the previous function.

4. Now we'll create the OnPickup function to cover what happens when we want to pick up an object, which is a very common interaction in VR. It has the same input and output as the last two functions.

5. Next is the OnDrop function; this will give us the opportunity to create additional functions when the player drops an object. It also has the same input and output as the last few functions.

6. The next three functions control the dragging of objects and allow us the opportunity to create even more gameplay with these actions. Create functions named OnDrag, OnDragStart, and OnDragEnd. They have the same input and output as all of the other functions that we've created here so far.

7. Finally, here's one that's different! Create a new function and name it CanPickUp. This function controls a Boolean that determines whether something is allowed to be picked up. It only has one output: a Boolean with the name PickUp.

8. This is the last one. Create one more function. This one is named OnUse and allows us to create objects that can be used as power ups. OnUse has input and output identical to OnHover.

We now have a second interface that allows us as designers as much freedom to create interactions as we have imagination. To test out our new player abilities, let's build a basic cube that can be interacted with in several different ways:

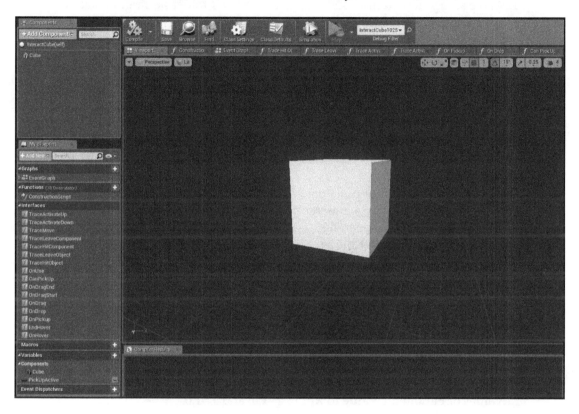

InteractCube with interface

To test our systems (and have a little fun), we're going to create a cube that utilizes many of the new functions that we've created in this chapter:

1. Make sure you're in the `Server17\Blueprints` folder and right-click in the **Content Browser** to create a new **Blueprint Class**. Choose **Actor** in the **Pick Parent Class** menu and name our new blueprint `InteractCube`.

2. Click the **Add Component** button in the **Components** panel and choose the **Cube** option from the **Common** section of the menu. In the **Details** panel, find the **Scale** values near the top and set the values so that **X=0.3, Y=0.3, and Z=0.3**.

3. It's time to add the interfaces. Click the **Class Defaults** button at the top of the screen. In the **Details** panel, click the **Add** button in the **Interfaces** section. Search for and add both the **Object Interaction Interface** and the **Button Interaction Interface**.

4. Now we have a load of functions to play with! Let's start with a way to tell when the cube is being hit by a line trace. Open the **Interfaces** section of the **My Blueprints** panel and open the `TraceHitObject` function. Right-click in the blueprint and search for the set **Vector Parameter Value (Cube)** on the **Materials** node. This node allows us to access the **Color** parameter on the cube's default material. Connect it to the function node and the **Return** node. Next, set the value of **Parameter Name** to **Color**. Finally, let's turn the cube red by changing the **Parameter Value X** value to 1.0. Now the cube will turn red when hit by a line trace!

5. Let's set the color back to white when the line trace leaves the cube. Double-click the `TraceLeaveObject` function in the **Interfaces** menu. Grab the same set **Vector Parameter Value (Cube)** node we used before, only, this time, set the values of **Parameter Value** to **X=1.0, Y=1.0, and Z=1.0**.

6. Having fun yet? Let's open the `TraceActivateDown` function from the **Interfaces** menu. Using the same preceding technique, create the **Set Vector Parameter Value (Cube)** node, type in the **Color** for the **Parameter Name**, and set the values of **Parameter Value** to **X=0, Y=1.0, and Z=0**. Our cube now turns green when we click the button to interact with it!

7. If we use `TraceActivateDown`, we should probably use `TraceActivateUp`. Let's set it up to change the color back to red when we release the button. Open the function and create another set **Vector Parameter Value (Cube)** node. Wire it into the function, set the value of **Parameter Name** to **Color**, and change the values of **Parameter Value** to **X=1.0, Y=0, and Z=0**.

Want to have a little more fun with our functions? Use the **Add Impulse** node where the target of the node is a **Scene Component** to create a sudden upward acceleration. Replace one of the set **Vector Parameter Value** nodes with **Add Impulse** and change the **Z** value of the **Impulse parameter** to **5000**. Make sure to turn on the checkbox for **Velocity Change**. This will shoot the cube skyward when the button is pressed or released!

8. How about we try the cube able to be picked up and thrown? To create this mechanism, we'll have Unreal simulate physics on our cube and then toggle this feature off and on when we pick up and drop the cube. Open the OnPickup and OnDrop functions. In OnPickup, right-click in the blueprint and search for the node set **Simulate Physics (Cube)**. Wire the execution input and output the the function node and the **Return** node, as it'll be the only node we use in this function. This will disable the physics when the cube is picked up so it won't fall out of the player's hands or exhibit other strange behavior. Now open OnDrop and create another copy of set **Simulate Physics (Cube)**. This time, turn on the checkbox next to the option to **Simulate Physics** on the node. This will enable the physics when the cube is dropped so it behaves the way we intend. Finally, head back to the **Viewport** tab and click on the cube. Check the **Details** panel to make sure the **Simulate Physics** option is turned on. If it's not, enable it.

9. There's one more function to set up. Go back to the **Interfaces** section of the **My Blueprints** panel and open the CanPickUp function. To make it so we can toggle this feature on and off, we're going to need a Boolean that we can toggle. In the **Variables** section, click the + button and create a new Boolean variable named PickUpActive. Back in the CanPickUp function, drag in a copy of our new variable and choose get from the menu. Plug the output of PickUpActive into the PickUp input on the **Return** node.

To make use of these new functions, we'll need to set up a way to call them in the **Interaction Component**, as well as map them to buttons in `Server17PlayerPawn`. This is exactly like what we did when we created the Object Interaction Interface earlier in this chapter. Head back to the **Content Browser** and open the **Interaction Component**:

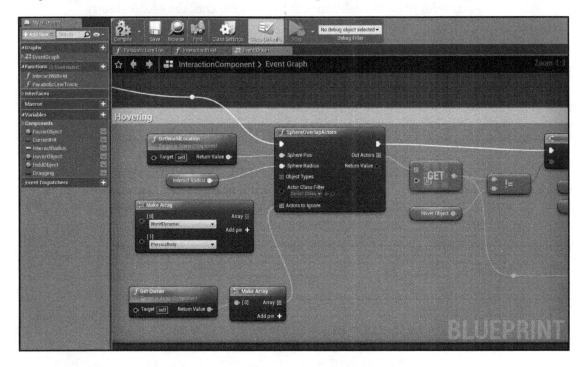

The Hover interaction component code

1. Inside the **Interaction Component**, we need to add some of the new player functionality, but the current code doesn't allow for that kind of expansion. To change that, we're going to use a **Sequence** node. The **Sequence** node is a flow-control node that implements the code connected to each of its output pins in order. To implement our new functions, we'll want to add the **Sequence** node after the **Gate**. Right-click in the blueprint and search for the **Sequence** node. Once created, click the **Add Pin** button in the bottom-left portion of the node. This will add an additional execution output. Connect the **Sequence** right after the **Gate** and connect the **Parabolic Line Trace** node to the execution output labeled **Then 0**.

2. Before we begin implementing the **Hover**, **Drag**, and **Pickup** features, we'll need a few more variables. Click the + button in **Variables** section of the **My Blueprint** panel and create a new **Float** variable named `InteractRadius`. Compile the blueprint and give it a default value of **10**. Next, create two variables of the type **Actor**, one named `HoverObject` and the other named `HeldObject`. Finally, create one more Boolean variable and name it `Dragging`.

3. Let's start by implementing the **Hovering** and **Dragging** behavior. Drag an execute line from the **Then 1** output on our new **Sequence** node and drop it in a clear area of the blueprint. The node we're looking for is called **SphereOverlapActors** and is designed to return the objects that it detects within a specific radius.

4. **SphereOverlapActors** needs four different input values. The first is **Sphere Position** (or **Pos**). We want the sphere to detect from wherever the interaction component is located. Drag a line from the **Sphere Pos** input and drop it. Search for the **GetWordlocation** node. This will give us an input of where the interaction components are in world space.

5. For the next input, grab a copy of our **InteractRadius** variable and choose **Get** from the menu. This will give a 10 cm detection radius for our interactions and make that radius easily adjustable through the variable.

6. Now we want to filter what the player can interact with. Drag a line off the **Object Types** input and search for the **Make Array** node. Click the **Add Pin** button on the node and use the two drop-down menus to choose the **WorldDynamic** and **PhysicsBody** options.

7. Finally, we want the player to ignore anything classified as itself so one motion controller can't interact with the other motion controller, for example. Right-click in the blueprint and use the search box to find the **Get Owner** node. This will return a reference to the player as an **Actor**. Since **SphereOverlapActors** only accepts an array as an input for **Actors To Ignore**, we'll need to insert the output from **Get Owner** into an array. Drag off from the **Return** value on **Get Owner** and drop it. Find the **Make Array** node and plug the resulting array into the final input on **SphereOverlapActors**.

8. **SphereOverlapActors** will now return an array of objects that match our criteria. With the output, we need to do a quick check to see whether the **HoverObject** we've stored in the variable is the same as the one we just took in. If they're the same, there's no reason to proceed; this will save us a bit of performance. Drag off the **Out Actors** output and search for the **Get** node. This will retrieve the item from the area at index 0 (the array should only contain one object). Next, get a reference to our **HoverObject** variable. Finally, to compare them, drag off the **HoverObject** variable and search for the **NotEqual** node. One input should be our **HoverObject** and the other should be the output of our **Get** node:

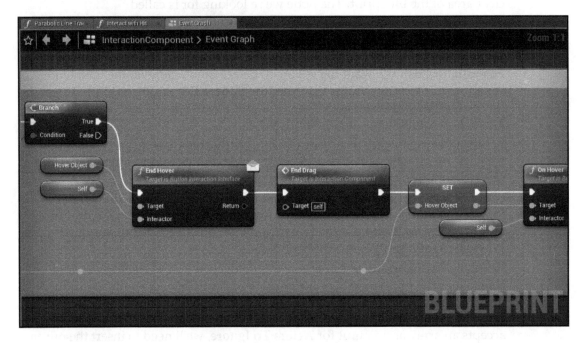

The second part of the Hover code

9. **NotEqual** will return a Boolean, so we'll need a **Branch** to continue. Connect the **Branch** to the execution output from the **SphereOverlapActors** node. The condition will be the result of the **NotEqual** node and we'll move forward only if it's **True**.

10. If our comparison is **True** and the two objects aren't the same, we're going to need to end the hovering behavior on the current object and set up the hovering or dragging behavior to work with the new object. Drag off from the **True** output on the **Branch** and search for our **EndHover** function from our Button Interaction Interface. Get a copy of our **HoverObject** variable and plug that into the **Target** input and use a **Reference to Self** as the **Interactor** input.

11. Next, create a copy of our **EndDrag** function and connect it to the execution output from our **EndHover** node.

12. Now we need to update the **HoverObject** variable with the new object we're hovering over. Drag in a copy of **HoverObject** and choose **Set** from the menu. The input will be the output from our **Get** node from earlier.

13. Lastly, we'll call the `OnHover` function to complete the sequence. Create a copy of our `OnHover` function and connect that to the execute output from the set **HoverObject**. The variable output from set the **HoverObject** can be used as the Target. Use a **Reference** to **Self** as as the **Interactor** input.

Our hovering code allows us to detect what the player might be reaching out for or holding their hand over, such as a button or an other component. Next, we'll tackle **Dragging**:

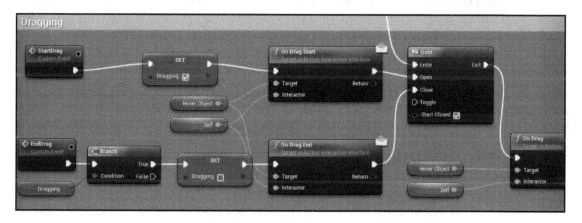

Dragging code

For **Dragging**, we'll need to create two **Custom Events** that can be called from outside the blueprint. This is exactly the same technique we used to implement our **ActivateUp** and **ActivateDown** behavior earlier:

1. To start, we'll create two **Custom Events**. Right-click in the blueprint and choose the **Add Custom Event** option. Name the first one `StartDrag` and the second one `EndDrag`.

2. For both of our new events, we basically want to turn our **Dragging** Boolean on and off while calling our **OnDragStart** and **OnDragEnd** functions. Let's start with **StartDrag**. Grab a copy of our **Dragging** variable and choose **Set** from the menu. Connect the execution output from our event to set **Dragging** and click the checkbox on the node to set it to **True**.

3. Now we'll call our **OnDragStart** function. Drag a copy of **OnDragStart** into the blueprint from the **Interfaces** section of **My Blueprint** and connect an execution line from set **Dragging**. Plug in a copy of our **HoverObject** variable as the **Target** and use a **Reference** to **Self** as the **Interactor**.

4. Next, we can work with our **EndDrag** custom event. The first step is to check to see whether our **Dragging** Boolean is **True**; if it is, then we can end the current drag. Create a new **Branch** node and connect the execute output from our event to it. Get a copy of **Dragging** and connect this to the **Condition** input on the **Branch**.

5. If **Dragging** is **True**, we need to update the variable and end the drag. Create another copy of **Dragging**, only this time choose **Set** from the menu and connect the **True** output from the **Branch** to it. Make sure the checkbox on **Dragging** is clear.

6. It's time to create a copy of our **OnDragEnd** function. Connect the execute output from set **Dragging** to the execute input on our new node. Just as we did for **OnDragStart** earlier, connect **HoverObject** as our **Target** and use a **Reference** to **Self** as the **Interactor**.

7. It's time to bring these two sequences together. We'll use a **Gate** to control whether or not something can be dragged with our custom events controlling whether the **Gate** is open or closed. Create a new **Gate** node and connect the output from **OnDragStart** to the **Open** input and bring in the output from **OnDragEnd** into the **Close** input. We'll connect the **Enter** input to the **Then 2** input on our **Sequence** node from earlier.

8. The final step to completing the drag is calling the **OnDrag** function. Create a copy and connect it to the **Exit** output from our **Gate** node we created in the last step. Just as we did for our previous drag functions, we'll connect a copy of our **HoverObject** variable to the **Target** input and plug in a **Reference** to **Self** as the **Interactor**.

We can now drag objects! Such a behavior might be useful in programming levers and other similar pieces that can be moved but not necessarily picked up. Speaking of picking up, the next feature we'll tackle is the ability to pick things up and throw them. Much like hovering or dragging, there's a similar trick to the pick-up-and drop behavior that happens behind the scenes. Most of the objects, but not all, will start with their **Simulate Physics** option enabled. The trick is this: when the object is picked up in VR, we'll attach the object to the player's hand so it can't get away from them. We will also disable the physics on the object (we set this up earlier in the **OnPickup** function of our **InteractCube**). When we put down the object, we detach it from the player and re-enable the physics. Since the player never sees any of the changes, it looks to them as if they just picked up the object and then put it down. Cool, huh?

Let's build it:

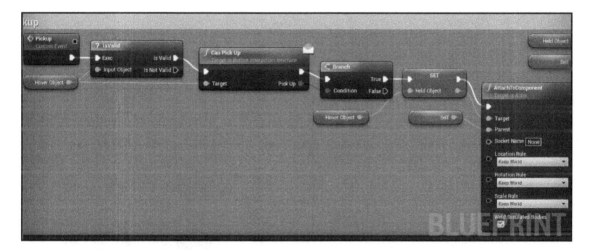

Pickup code

Just as we did for the dragging behavior, we'll start by creating two custom events: one for **Pickup** and one for **Drop**:

1. Right-click in our blueprint and create two new custom events with the **Add Custom Event** option. Name the first `Pickup` and the second `Drop`.

2. We'll start by building the pickup behavior. We need to start by checking whether the object the player is hovering over is a valid object. Right-click in the blueprint and search for the **IsValid** node. The version we need is marked with a question mark as its icon. Connect it to our **Pickup** event and create a copy of our **HoverObject** variable, which will serve as the input for the **Input** object pin on the node.

3. Now that we know whether the object is real (in a manner of speaking), we can check to see whether we can pick it up! Create a copy of our **CanPickUp** function and connect **HoverObject** as the **Target**. This will return a **True** or **False**, which will determine whether the player can pick up the object.

4. Next, we need a **Branch** to process the Boolean from **CanPickUp**. We only want the player to pick things up if this is **True**. Create a new **Branch** node and connect it to the execute output from **CanPickUp**. The **Condition** input will be the **PickUp** output from **CanPickUp**.

5. We know now whether the object is real. We also know whether we're allowed to pickup it. Now it's the time to do the heavy lifting. Create a copy of our **HeldObject** variable and choose set from the menu. The input for **Set HeldObject** will be the current value of **HoverObject**.

6. Next, create a copy of the **AttachToComponent** node, making sure we're using the **Target is Actor** version. Connect it to the output of the set **HeldObject**. Also, pass the variable output of set **HeldObject** into the **Target** input on **AttachToComponent**. Now create a **Reference** to **Self** and plug that into the **Parent** input. Lastly, set the **Location Rule**, **Rotation Rule**, and **Scale Rule** settings in the node to the **Keep World** option. This will maintain the basic attributes of the object we pick up so that, when we drop it, everything will remain the same.

7. The next step is to call our **OnPickup** function to trigger any special behaviors we might want for that object. Create a copy of **OnPickup** and connect the output from **AttachToComponent** to it. Connect a copy of the **HeldObject** variable to the Target input and use a **Reference** to **Self** as the **Interactor**.

8. Now that we have the ability to pick things up and drop them, we may want the player to be able to use something they're hovering over. To create this behavior, we'll need to create a custom event named **UseHovered**. Next, create a copy of our `OnUse` function and connect it to our custom event. Get a copy of our **HoverObject** variable to use as the **Target**. Finish the node with a **Reference** to **Self** to use as the **Interactor**:

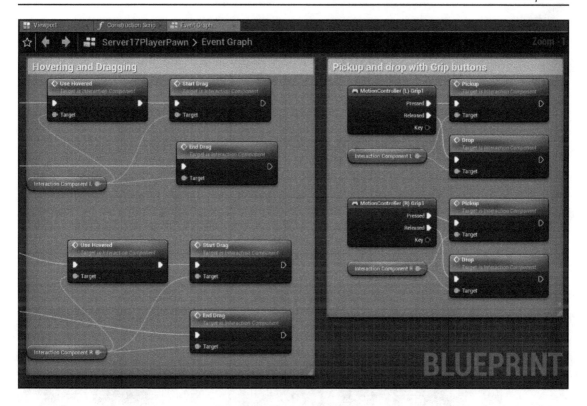

Pickup/Drop and Hover/Drag code in player pawn

9. To be able to utilize our new behaviors (**Hover**, **Drag**, **Pickup**, and **Drop**), we'll need to map them to buttons on the player's motion controller. Let's add hover and drag to the triggers. Open `Server17PlayerPawn` and find where we mapped **ActivateUp** and **ActivateDown** to the motion controller triggers. We'll start with the left trigger. Extend an execute line from **ActivateDown** and drop it to search for our **UseHovered** function (referencing the left interaction component). Next, drag off the reference to **InteractionComponent_L** and search for the **StartDrag** function. Connect this to the execute output on the **UseHovered** function. Finish by dragging off the reference to **InteractionComponent_L** again and searching for **EndDrag**. We'll connect this to the execution output from **ActivateUp**. Now we can use hovered objects, as well as start and end drag sequences!

10. Repeat the same process for the right motion controller.

11. Finally, it's time to map the pickup and drop behaviors. Many games map this type of behavior to the grip buttons as players seem to naturally gravitate toward using these buttons, for this interaction. Right-click in the blueprint and search for the **MotionController L Grip1** event. Drag an execution line from the Pressed output and search for our **Pickup** function (referencing the left interaction component). Now drag off the reference to **InteractionComponent_L** and search for the **Drop** function. Connect this new function to the **Released** output on the event. As before, repeat this process for the right motion controller as well.

Done! To test the behavior, let's drop a few of these wonderful cubes in our level and test their functionality. Pick them up, throw them, and watch them change color. Pretty cool, right? Just think about all of the possibilities for gameplay with the power you now hold within this cube. It gives you ideas, doesn't it? Before we get to implementing those ideas, why don't we add one more tool to our toolbox in the form of a button our players can press:

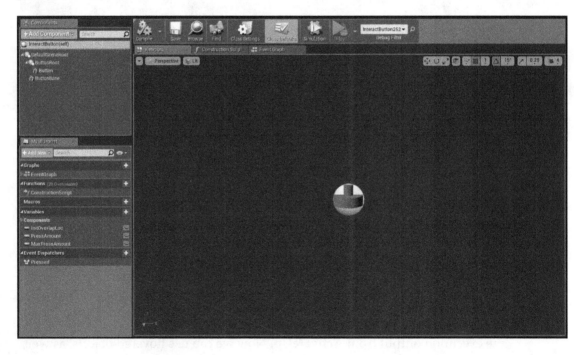

Button press code

We can start building our button in the **Viewport**:

1. Our button will be built from three different components. In the **Viewport** tab, click the **Add Component** button and create a new **Scene Component**. Name this ButtonRoot . Next, create a **Cylinder** component and name it Button. We'll need to scale the cylinder down a bit so change the **X**, **Y**, and **Z** values for the **Scale** property to 0.05. Also, change its **Collision Preset** to **OverlapAllDynamic**. Make sure the button is a child of the **ButtonRoot**. Lastly, create one more **Cylinder** component named ButtonBase and make sure that it's a child of the **Default Scene Root**. We'll need to change the **Scale** property here too. Change the scale values to **X=0.15**, **Y=0.15**, and **Z=0.05**. Finally, set its **Collision Preset** to **NoCollision**.

2. Now that the visual components have been created, we can move on to the blueprint. We want to create a button that animates a bit when the player hovers their hand on it, and, for that, we'll need a few variables. The first we'll create is named InitOverlapLoc of the type **Vector**. This will store the location where the player's hand started overlapping. The second is MaxPressAmout of the type **Float**. This will be an adjustable variable so that we can fine tune how much the player needs to press the button for it to fire. Compile the blueprint and set the default value of this variable to **4**. The third variable we need is named PressAmount of the type **Float**. This will store the amount that the player has pressed the button. Lastly, we need to store the name of the component that over lapped the button. Create one more variable and name it OverlapComponent. Make sure its type is **Primitive Component**.

3. We're going to start our first code sequence with two events. Click on the **Button** component we created earlier and head to the **Details** panel. Near the very bottom of the list in the **Events** section of the menu is a collection of buttons that allows you to create almost every event compatible with our **Button**. We need to create two: **OnComponentBeginOverlap** and **OnComponentEndOverlap**. This will detect when the player's hand is pressing the button.

4. **OnComponentBeginOverlap** feels like a good place to start, since it's the event that kicks everything off. The first step is to check and see whether the component overlapping the button is valid. Create a copy of the **IsValid** node (remember the one with the question mark?). Connect it to the event and get a copy of our **OverlapComponent** variable to be pluged into the **Input Object** pin.

5. If our **OverlapComponent** isn't valid (meaning the variable is empty), we need to store whatever overlapped the button as our new value for **OverlapComponent**. Grab another copy of **OverlapComponent**, only, this time, choose **Set** from the menu. The input for the new node will be the **Other Comp** input from the event node.

6. With the **OverlapComponent** set, we now also need to set its location in our **InitOverlapLoc** variable. Right-click in the blueprint and grab a copy of the **GetWorldLocation** node where the target of the node is a **Scene Component**. Connect the execute input to the execute output of set **OverlapComponent**. Have the variable input for **GetWorldLocation** by the variable output for the set **OverlapComponent**.

7. Now we need to store the new location in **InitOverlapLoc**. Create a new set **InitOverlapLoc** node. The variable input for this new node will be the output from **GetWorldLocation**. Don't forget to connect the execute connection!

8. It's time to tackle the **OnComponentEndOverlap** event. When we end the overlap, all we want to do is check to see whether the object that was removed from overlapping is the same that we've stored in the **OverlapComponent** variable and whether it's we want to clear that variable. Start the sequence by creating a **Branch** and connecting it to the execution output of the event. To compare our objects, create a copy of the **Equals** (object) node. The top input with be the **OtherComp** output from the event. The bottom will be a copy of our **OverlapComponent** variable. Finally, connect the Boolean output from the **Equals** node to the **Condition** input on the **Branch**.

9. For the final step in this sequence, create a copy of **OverlapComponent** and choose **Set** from the menu. Connect it to the **True** execution output on the **Branch**. We'll leave its variable input blank so that we can clear its value.

10. The next step in our code is to build the nodes that will control the short animation. We begin with the **Event Tick** node. Next, right-click and create a **Sequence** node, since this will be a two-step process. Connect the **Sequence** to the execute output from **Even Tick**:

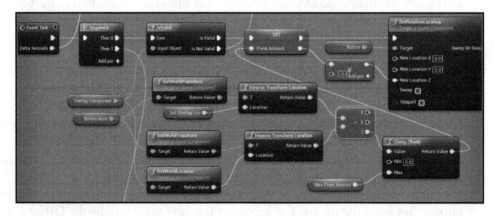

Button down code

11. Dragging off the **Then 0** output, drop the connection and use the search box to find the **IsValid** node (remember to use the one marked with a **?** in the menu). The **Input Object** we'll be checking this time will be a copy of our **OverlapComponent**. We'll use this setup to determine whether the player is still overlapping with the button. If they are, we'll animate the button going down. If they aren't, we'll animate the button, returning to the original position.

12. Next, drag in a copy of our **PressAmount** variable and choose the **Set** option from the menu. Connect this to the **IsValid** output. We'll leave its variable input blank for now.

13. To do the actual animating, we'll need to create a copy of a **SetRelativeLocation** node. Connect its execute input to the execute output from the set **PressAmount** and use a reference to the **Button** component as the **Target**.

14. With the basics of the code set up for the animation, it's time to do some quick math. Pressing a **Button** is a basic motion that involves moving the button component moving up and down in the Z axis when the player overlaps it. To figure out how far the button needs to travel, we'll take the distance the overlapping actor has traveled and subtract it from the initial position of that same actor. We'll compare that distance to our **MaxPressAmount** to determine whether the button has been truly pressed. This will all be calculated relative to the position of the button to ensure that it'll work in whatever situation you decide to use it. We'll start with converting our stored **InitOverlapLoc** value to be in relation to the button. Get a reference to the **ButtonBase** from the **Components** panel, drag a connection off of it, and drop it to open the search menu. Create a copy of **GetWorldTransform**.

15. Dragging a line from the return value of **GetWorldTransform**, drop the connection, and search for the **InverseTransformLocation** node. This node is designed to take in a location and convert it from **World Space** over into **Local Space**, based on the transform that we supply. In this case, we're converting the initial overlap location to be relative to the **ButtonBase**. Get a copy of our **InitOverlapLoc** variable and connect that to the **Location** input.

16. Now create a `Vector - Vector` node and take the **Return** value of the **InverseTransformLocation** and plug that into the top input. We'll calculate the second value in the following steps.

17. Drag another connection off the reference to **ButtonBase** and create another copy of **GetWorldTransform** and another copy of **InverseTransformLocation**.

18. This time, we'll need to get the location of the component we've stored in **OverlapComponent**. Get a copy of the **OverlapComponent** variable and drag a connection off it. Drop it and search for **GetWorldLocation**. The **Return Value** of this node will be the **Location** input on the copy of the **InverseTransformLocation** we created in *step 17*. The **Return Value** of this **InverseTransformLocation** can now be connected to the lower input on our `Vector - Vector`.

19. Since the button only travels in the Z axis, we're only interested in the Z output of the subtraction node. Right-click on the output of the `Vector - Vector` and split the struct pin.

20. To make sure the Z value doesn't go outside what we need, we're going to use a **Clamp** node to limit it. A **Clamp** node takes in a value and tells it that it can only be between a certain minimum and maximum. In this case, we're going to bring in the Z value and not let it go lower than zero or higher than our **MaxPressAmount**. Right-click and create a **Clamp** (float) node. Use the Z ouput from our `Vector - Vector` as the **Value** input and a copy of our **MaxPressAmount** variable as the **Max**. We should leave the minimum value at **0**.

21. We're almost there! Our clamped float value is now ready to become the input for the set **PressAmount** node we created earlier. Connect the output of the **Clamp** to the set **PressAmount** input.

22. Since the button will always be moving down to show that it's being pressed, the value we need to pass into our **SetRelativeLocation** node should be negative. Take the variable output from set **PressAmount**, drag off from it, and create a `Float * Float` node. Set the second value to **-1.0**.

23. To finish the animation, right-click on the **New Location** input on the **SetRelativeLocation** and split the struct. Connect the output from Float * Float and connect to the **New Location** Z input:

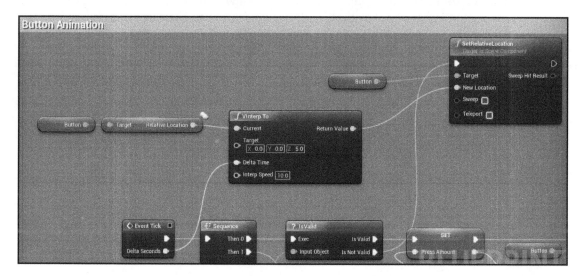

Code that returns the button to the start position

24. Once the overlap is complete, we'll need to move the button back to its original location. Head back to the **IsValid** that we created back in *step 11* and drag a connection of the **IsNotValid** output, drop it, and search for a copy of the node **SetRelativeLocation**. Set a reference to our **Button** component as the Target.

25. Right-click in the blueprint and search for the **VinterpTo**. This will help the button achieve a smooth animation back to an unpressed state. To fill the **Current** input, grab a reference to the **Button** component and drag a connection off it. Drop and search for a **GetRelativeLocation** node. Plug the output from this node into the **Current** input.

26. To fill the **Delta Time** input, connect the **Delta Time** value from the **Event Tick** node.

27. Finally, connect the **Return Value** from **VinterpTo** to the **New Location** input on **SetRelativeLocation**.

The last thing needed to finish the button is a way to process what happens when the button is pressed. For that, we'll use an **Event Dispatcher**. By using an **Event Dispatcher**, we can bind different commands to the button, depending on what we need it for, leaving us with a flexible and reusable system:

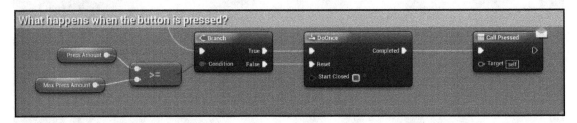

What happens when it's pressed?

To continue, drag off the **Then 1** output on our **Sequence** node and create a new **Branch**:

28. It's now time to compare the amount we have pressed the button to the max press amount. Right-click and create a `Float >= Float` node. Get a copy of **PressAmount** and connect that to the top input. Get a copy of **MaxPressAmount** and connect that to the bottom input. Lastly, plug the output of the node into the **Condition** input on the **Branch**.

29. Now create a **DoOnce** node. This node stops something from happening again until it has been reset. We'll plug the **True** output from the **Branch** into the execute input and the **False** output into the **Reset** input.

30. Finally, create an **Event Dispatcher**. Find the **Event Dispatchers** section of the My Blueprint panel and click the + button. Name the new dispatcher Pressed. Back in the blueprint, drag off the **Completed** output of **DoOnce** and search for the **Call Pressed** node.

31. The last step in implementing our button-press behavior is to add some code to the interaction component.

We now have a working button that the player can mash in VR. To test the feature, drop a copy of our button into the level where you can press it and open the **Level Blueprint**. We are going to build from the **Event BeginPlay** node that should be present in the blueprint by default. If it isn't there, go ahead and drop one in.

Right-click in the blueprint and create a reference to the **InteractButton** that's in the level. Drag off from the output and search for the **AssignPressed** node and connect the execute output from the event to its input. This will allow you to assign a custom event to **Pressed**. It can be anything you want! I created a simple way to end the level in the previous screenshot.

Wow! We've come a long way from where we began. The player now has hands. They can use them to interact with the world around them. They can touch, pick up, throw, press buttons, and anything else that we can dream up. They can also teleport around the level to explore whatever we decide to create—and all of this with controls in place so that they may only do these things with whatever we as the designers let them. It's time to put that power to good use.

Remember the puzzle box we designed at the beginning of the section? We now have all of the pieces we need to make this a reality. Since it's a prototype, we're going to build the box out of static mesh components and another type of component called a **Child Actor**. **Child Actors** are copies of class blueprints and allow us to build objects within a class blueprint out of other actors, meaning that we can piece together our simple puzzle box with **Box** components, copies of our **InteractCube**, and a couple copies of **InteractButton**:

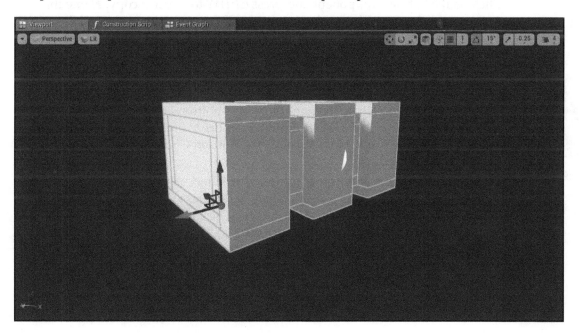

Building the PuzzleCubeTest

Start by creating a new **Class Blueprint**:

1. Right-click in the `Server17\Blueprint` folder in the **Content Browser** and create a new **Class Blueprint** based on **Actor**. Name this new blueprint **PuzzleCubeTest**, since this puzzle cube represents our first prototype. Double-click it to open it.

2. Let's create the visual components. The best place to start would be with the non-interactive components first. In the **Components** section of **My Blueprints**, click the **Add Components** button, and create a new **Box** component. Change the **Scale** properties **X=1.0**, **Y=2.0**, and **Z=0.1**. Name this component `Bottom`.

3. Create another **Box** component and name it `RightSide`. Change the **Scale** properties **X=0.5**, **Y=2.0**, and **Z=0.1** and rotate it 90 degrees around the *Y* axis. Line it up along the right edge of the bottom component.

4. Select the **Right** component and press *Ctrl + W*. This will create a copy that you can align with the left edge of the bottom piece. Name this new piece `LeftSide`. Change its Y **Scale** property to 1.5. This space will allow for the hidden compartment in the back.

5. Click on the bottom component and press *Ctrl+W* to create a copy. Name this new component **Top**. Move this component 60 cm up in the positive *Z* direction.

6. The box is slowly coming together, but now we need a back plate to finish the enclosure. Create a new **Box** component and change the **Scale** property to **X=0.9**, **Y=0.5**, and **Z=0.1**. Name it **BackPlate**. Finally, rotate it 90 degrees around the *X* axis.

7. Now we're going to create the non-interactive bottom and top supports. Create a new **Box** component and name it **BottomSupport_1**. Set the **Scale** property to **X=0.5**, **Y=1.25**, and **Z=0.1**. Move it below the **Bottom Component** and align it with the front and side edges.

8. With **BottomSupport_1** selected, press *Ctrl + W* and name this new component `BottomSupport_2`. Rotate it 90 degrees around the *Z* axis and move it back to the center of the bottom of the box. The easy way to do this would be to set the *Y* value of its location property back to 0.

9. Create another copy of **BottomSupport_1** and name it **BottomSupport_3**. Rotate it 90 around the *Z* axis and align this component with the back edge of the bottom component.

10. Select all of the **BottomSupport** components in the **Components** list by clicking the first one and holding *Ctrl* while selecting the other two. If necessary, rotate the components 90 degrees so that they're back in the correct orientation. Then move them 80 cm up in the *Z* axis so that their bottom edges align with the top edge of the **Top** component. Name them `TopSupport_1`, `TopSupport_2`, and `TopSupport_3`.

11. To give one of our buttons inside the box a surface to sit on, we're going to create one more non-interactive component. Click on the **BackPlate** component and create a copy with *Ctrl + W*. Name this new component `MiddlePlate` and make the value of it's **Location** property **X=0**, **Y=60**, and **Z=30**.

12. To create the interactive surfaces in our puzzle box, we're going utilize **Child Actor** components, which will be copies of our **InteractCube** object. This will allow us to have all of the functionality that we programmed into **InteractCube** and utilize them as components of our puzzle box without reprogramming them in a new component (though we may want to in the future). Create a new **Child Actor** component and name it `SideDecoy_R1`. In the **Details** panel, set the **Child Actor** class property to **InteractCube**. Se the **Scale** value to **X=0.5, Y=0.13**, and **Z=0.7** and rotate it 90 degrees around the *Z* axis. Move this component into position in between the first set of the top and bottom supports on the right side, aligned to the front edge of the **RightSide** component.

13. Create a copy of **SideDecoy_R1** using *Ctrl + W* and name the new **Child Actor** `SideDecoy_R2`. Move it between the rear set of the top and bottom supports on the right side, aligned with the back edge of the **Right** component.

14. Now for the left side, create a copy of `SideDecoy_R1` using *Ctrl + W* and name the new **Child Actor** `SideDecoy_L1`. Move it to the left side of the box between the first set of top and bottom supports and align it with the front edge of the **LeftSide** component.

15. Make a copy of `SideDecoy_L1` and move it to the center set of the top and bottom supports.

16. The decoy components are there to divert the players attention while they look for the buttons to press to unlock the puzzle box. With them all in place, we can now add our interactive button components. On the right-hand side of our puzzle box, create a new **Child Actor** component and set the **Child Actor** class property to **InteractButton**. Name this new `Child Actor Button_Step1`. Lastly, move it to the center of the area between the middle top and bottom supports and align it with the surface of the **RightSide** component by rotating it -90 degrees around the *Y* axis. Players will need to uncover and find this button before they can open the front of the box.

17. Create a copy of **Button_Step1** with *Ctrl + W* and name the new component **Button_Step2**. Set the button's **Rotation** property to **X=0**, **Y=90**, and **Z=90**. Align this button with the center of our **MiddlePlate** component. This button will be found behind a plate that covers the front of the puzzle box that can only be removed after **Button_Step1** has been pressed.

18. Now let's cover up those buttons! Create a copy of **SideDecoy_R1** and name the new component `ButtonCover_Step1`. Move this new object to cover up **Button_Step1** by aligning it between the center set of the top and bottom supports on the right side.

19. To cover the front, we'll need a new **Child Actor** sized to fit that compartment. Create a new **Child Actor**, set the **Child Actor** class property to **InteractCube**, and name it `ButtonCover_Step2`. Set the value of the **Scale** property to **X=0.8**, **Y=0.5**, and **Z=0.1**. Rotate it around the *X* axis 90 degrees. Lastly, align it to cover **Button_Step2** and fit it flush with the front of the puzzle box. This will unlock after the player presses the first button.

20. There's one more cover. This one will cover the compartment we have in the back. Click on **SideDecoy_L2** and use *Ctrl + W* to create a copy of it. Name the new copy `CompartmentCover_Step3`. Align it between the back top and bottom supports to cover the compartment. This cover will unlock when the player presses the second button.

21. What good is a puzzle box if there's no prize at the end? Create one more **Child Actor** component and set the **Child Actor** class property to **InteractCube**. Name it **StolenData**. This will represent the prize the player is after. Set the value of the **Scale** property to **X=0.1**, **Y=0.1**, and **Z=0.1**. Place inside of rear compartment that we just covered with **CompartmentCover_Step3**.

22. There's one last detail. To make the **InteractCube** work as a stand-in for more detailed components that we'll create later, we need to open the **InteractCube** blueprint and turn off the **Simulate Physics** option. This will make it so the cubes won't have physics enabled by default, so the puzzle cube won't fall apart. Physics will still enable once the player has interacted with the cube.

Based on our design, the code for the prototype puzzle box needs to be able to do the following things:

- Disable the ability to pick up the button covers when we start
- Bind the correct button press events to our two buttons
- Enable the front button cover after button 1 has been pressed
- Enable the compartment cover after button 2 has been pressed

Disabling the components that we don't want the player to be able to interact with what could be accomplished by toggling their individual **PickUpActive** Boolean variables. This will leave all of their other functions available but make it so the player can't remove them before we want them to have that ability. To give them that ability, we can bind a couple of custom events to our two buttons that re-enable them after the buttons have been found and pressed. Let's head to the **Event Graph** of **PuzzleCubeTest** and get to work:

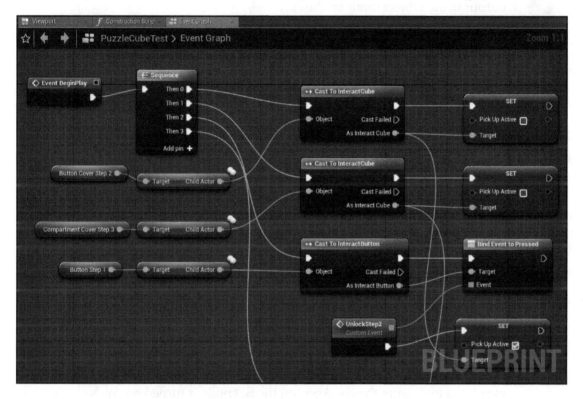

PuzzleBoxTest code

We'll build this code from the **Event BeginPlay** node:

1. Right-click in the blueprint and search for a **Sequence** node. We are going to use this to fire off the steps that we mentioned previously in the correct order. Click the **Add Pin** button on the node until we have four output pins to work with.

2. Start by dragging off the **Then 0** output and search for the **Cast To InteractCube** node. For the **Object** input on the cast, we need to reference our **Child Actor ButtonCover_Step2**. However, if we try to plug in a simple reference to it, the cast won't work correctly. To make sure it references the correct object, we need to add a **GetChildActor** node. Create a reference to **ButtonCover_Step2** and drag a connection from its output. Search for the **GetChildActor** node and connect its output to the **Object** input on the cast.

3. With the cast set up, we can now pretend to be the button cover and turn off its ability to be picked up. Drag a connection off the **As InteractCube** output and search for the set **PickUpActive**. On the set **PickUpActive** node, make sure the checkbox is turned off.

4. Let's repeat the process for **CompartmentCover_Step3**. Create the cast by dragging off the **Then 1** output on the **Sequence** and connecting a reference to the **Child Actor** version of **CompartmentCover_Step3** to the **Object** input through a **GetChildActor** node. As the child actor, set **PickUpActive** to false by turning off the checkbox on the **Set** node.

5. Next, we need to connect the button presses to a couple of custom events. Drag a connection off the **Then 2** output on the **Sequence** node and search for the node **Cast To InteractButton**. Use the same method as the previous one to create a reference to the child actor, **Button_Step1**, and connect that to the **Object** input on the cast. We'll use our event dispatcher we created as part of the button to connect a custom event to the pressing of the button. Drag a connection off the **As InteractButton** output and search for **Bind Event** to **Pressed**.

6. Create a new custom event and name it **UnlockStep2**. Drag a connection off the little box next to the event node's name and plug it into the event input on the Bind **Event to Pressed** node.

7. Drag a connection from the As **InteractCube** output from *step 3* and create a set **PickUpActive** node. Connect it to the execution output from the **UnlockStep2** event and make sure the checkbox on the **Set** node is turned on. We've now re-enabled **ButtonCover_Step2**.

8. Repeat the steps to set up the ability to re-enable **CompartmentCover_Step3**. Create a **Cast To InteractButton** node and pass in a reference to the child actor version of **Button_Step2**. As the button, create a **Bind Event** to **Pressed** node and connect it to a custom event named **UnlockStep3**. Drag off the **As InteractCube** output from *step 4* and create a set **PickUpActive** node. Make sure that the checkbox on this new node is set to on.

And there we have it, a working puzzle cube that takes three steps to solve. Using our teleport volumes, create a space where you can teleport around the box and then drop a copy of the puzzle box in the center. Move around it. Test the steps and see whether they work. Once everything is working, I have a challenge for you. When we started this section, I provided a sketch of the plan for the puzzle box, as well as a prototype level for the player to test it. Build the level and test your puzzle box in it. Interested in a greater challenge? Design and build your own puzzle cube and test level!

Building the first tool station

An integral part of the gameplay for *Server 17* is the idea of the Tool Station, a location located near the puzzle box that contains some type of tool, device, or hint-generator that can be used by the player to help solve the puzzle at hand. The tools at each station would vary from brute-force hacking tools that could solve a step of the puzzle at the cost of a time penalty, to a simple hint tool that could highlight the next piece the player has to interact with. For the prototype, we're going to design a simple rotation tool that will highlight how easy it is to use the tools that we created. Let's take a look at the prototype visuals:

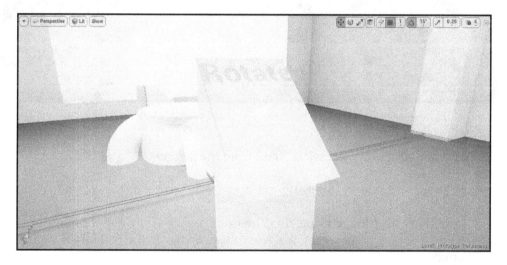

Prototype visuals

The build is relatively basic. Using the **Content Browser**, head to the `Shapes` folder of the **Starter Content** and grab yourself a cylinder. Use the **Scale** tool to shrink it by half. Then grab a **Wedge** shape and place that on top of the cylinder. Shrink this by half as well. I also used a **Text Render** to create the text you see in the image. The final piece to this tool station is a new class blueprint:

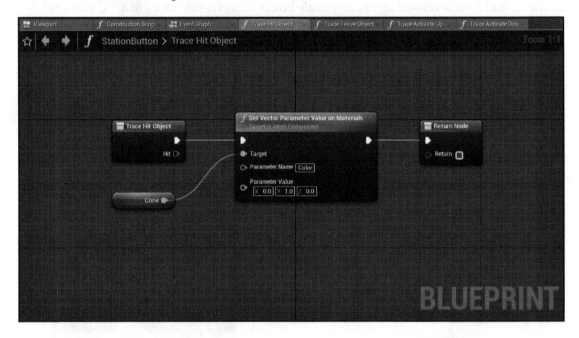

StationButton code

Create a new class **Blueprint** and select **Actor** from the menu:

1. Create the new class **Blueprint**, select the **Actor** class from the **Pick Parent Class** menu, and name it `StationButton`.
2. Similar to our **InteractCube**, this blueprint contains only one component. I used a **Cone** component; however, feel free to use whatever you feel might be appropriate.
3. Now, let's code this thing! To utilize some of the functions that we've spent this chapter creating, click on the **Class Defaults** button and find the **Interfaces** section in the **Details** panel. Click the **Add** button and choose our **Object Interaction** Interface.

4. With the interface added, head over to the **My Blueprint** panel and open the **Interfaces** section of the menu. Double-click and open the following functions: `TraceHitObject`, `TraceLeaveObject`, `TraceActivateUp`, and `TraceActivateDown`.

5. Let's start with `TraceHitObject`. This covers what happens when our line trace touches the object. Drag a reference to the **Cone** into the blueprint from the **Components** panel and drag a connection from it. Create a copy of the **SetVectorParameterValueOnMaterial** and connect it to the function node and **Return** node. Set the value of the **Parameter Name** field to **Color**. Finally, set the *Y* value of the **Parameter Value** input to **1.0**. This will highlight the button **Green** when we land a trace on it.

6. For `TraceLeaveObject`, we'll have to create a variable that can store whether or not our button is being used. Head over to the **Variables** section of **My Blueprint** and create a new Boolean variable. Name it `ButtonPressed` and set its default value to **False**. Along with changing the color of the button back to the default white, we want to make sure the button no longer registers as pressed if it's no longer being touched by a line trace. Repeat the preceding step to create the **SetVectorParameterValueOnMaterial** node and set the value of the **Parameter Value** input to **X=1.0**, **Y=1.0**, and **Z=1.0**. This will set the button color back to white. After **SetVectorParameterValueOnMaterial**, connect a set **ButtonPressed** node and make sure the checkbox is set to off. Connect that to the output of **SetVectorParameterValueOnMaterial** and the **ReturnNode**.

7. Now, let's move on to `TraceActivateDown`. When the player activates the button, all we want to do is set **ButtonPressed** to **True**. We'll handle the rotating in the level blueprint. Connect a copy of the set **ButtonPressed** to the function. Make sure the checkbox on the node is turned on. After the **Set** node, create another copy of **SetVectorParameterValueOnMaterial** using the **Cone** as the **Target**. Set it up the same way as we did in the previous steps in this section and set the *X* value of the **Parameter Value** input to **1.0**. This will turn the button red when it's used.

8. Lastly, we have `TraceActivateUp`. When the player releases the trigger, we need to change the color back to green (the color it is when getting hit by a line trace) and change **ButtonPressed** back to false. Connect a copy of **SetVectorParameterValueOnMaterial** to the function node, set it up as we have in previous steps, and set the *Y* value of the **Parameter Value** input to **1.0**. Connect a copy of set **ButtonPressed** to the output of the **SetVectorParameterValueOnMaterial** node and connect its output to the **Return** node, making sure the checkbox is set to off.

9. Back in our level, add a copy of **StationButton** to the tools station that we've created and name it **StationButton_Rotate**.

To make the puzzle box rotate when our station button is pressed, we're going to build a bit of functionality into the level blueprint, since this ability is limited to the prototype level. Open the **Level Blueprint** using the **Blueprints** button:

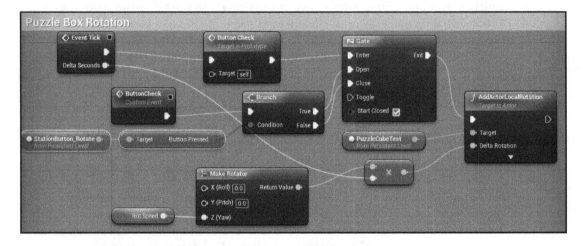

The level blueprint code

We'll start to build this sequence with a custom event:

1. Right-click in the blueprint and create a new custom event. We are going to name it **ButtonCheck**.
2. Next, right-click and create a new **Branch** node. This will read whether the button has been pressed. Create a reference to our **StationButton_Rotate** and drag a connection from it. Drop it and search for **Get ButtonPressed**. Connect the output from this node to the **Condition** node on the **Branch**.
3. Now, create an **Event Tick** node. We want the game to check every frame if the button is being pressed. Drag a connection from the event and search for our **ButtonCheck** function to create a copy of it.

4. As we've done for previous buttons, we're going to use a **Gate** to control whether the code executes, based on whether **ButtonPressed** is **True** or **False**. Create a **Gate** node and connect the Enter input to the output from the **ButtonCheck** function. Connect the True output from our **Branch** to the **Open** input and the **False** output from the **Branch** to the **Close** input.

5. It's time to create the rotation. Create a new `Float` variable over in the **Variables** section of **My Blueprint** and name it **RotSpeed**. This will control how fast the puzzle cube rotates.

6. Next, right-click and search for the **Make Rotator** node. Connect a copy of **RotSpeed** to the **Z (Yaw)** input.

7. The last major node we need is **AddActorLocalRotation**. Connect it to the **Exit** output of our **Gate** node and use a reference to our puzzle cube in the level as the **Target**.

8. The **Delta Rotation** input needs a bit of math. Drag a connection from the output of **Make Rotator** and search for the **ScaleRotator** node. For the float input, use the **Delta Seconds** output from **Event Tick**. This will create a smooth rotation over time.

9. Finally, plug the output of our **ScaleRotator** node into the **Delta Rotation** input on the **AddActorLocalRotation**.

We now have rotation! Obviously, there's quite a bit more that can be done with the idea of hacking tools in *Server 17*, but this will work fine for our prototype stage. It looks as though this is finally coming together. There is one last gameplay element we still haven't created though: our level timer.

Building the Timer

In the world of *Server 17*, players hack corporate servers looking for valuable company secrets. However, those corporations don't just lie down and take it! Powerful system administrators, corporate hackers, and AI countermeasures mobilize to stop the player, giving them limited time to crack each server. To represent this in the game, we'll implement a level timer in the game that will cause the player to lose when it reaches zero. Since this is a only a prototype, we'll have the game quit when the timer is complete.

Since this is a gameplay element independent of any level, we'll build this feature in our custom game state. Head to our `Sever17\Blueprints` server and double-click the `S17GameState` to open it:

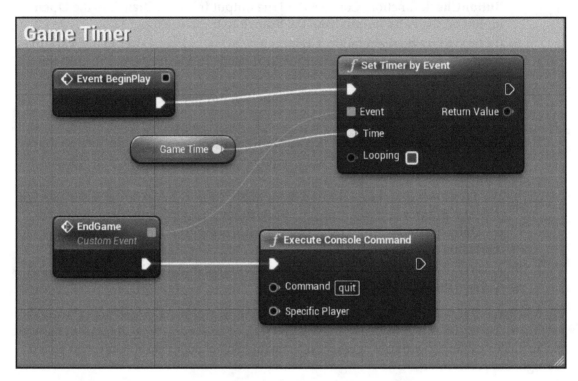

Game timer code setup in the Game State

Let's get started:

1. This feature makes user of the **Timer** system built into the **Blueprint** system. Using the **SetTimerByEvent** node, we can call a custom event when a timer (in seconds) completes. Start by creating a copy of the **Event BeginPlay** node and dragging an execute connection off the output. Search for the **SetTimerByEvent** node and select it from the menu.

2. Next, create a **Custom Event** named `EndGame`. Connect this custom event to the **Event** input on **SetTimerByEvent** by dragging a connection from the square pin next to the custom event's name and connecting to the input pin.

3. Dragging off the **EndGame** event, search for the **ExecuteConsoleCommand** node. In the **Command** field, type in the command `quit`.

4. To finish the sequence, we need to set a value for **Time** on **SetTimerByEvent**. To keep the system flexible, we'll create a variable for the game time that can easily be adjusted from outside the game state to take into account things such as level difficulty or story elements. Create a new `Float` variable and name it **GameTime**. Compile the blueprint and set the default value to 300. Get a copy of it and connect it to the **Time** input on **SetTimerByEvent**.

Awesome! Our intrepid players now have five minutes to complete our puzzle cube or be kicked out of the game. Feel free to adjust the default value of **GameTime** to whatever feels appropriate for your players or to adjust the challenge for yourself.

Summary

Wow! What a ride. We began this chapter with some interesting discussions about gameplay and ended it with creating a whole game prototype from scratch! In this chapter, we explored the many different types of gameplay that successfully implement the mechanics that VR is uniquely capable of. Using that knowledge, we designed our game elements to take advantage of the near one-to-one translation of player movement into the game and the ability to have the player interact with the world from a true first-person perspective. Through the rest of this chapter, we built all of our systems from scratch from hand interactions to VR buttons, and even a puzzle box for the player to solve within a time limit.

In the next chapter, we're going to expand our gameplay by discussing the user experience we've created so far and how we can improve that experience through the use of user interfaces. We'll talk about the use and viability of 2D and 3D elements within our game world and what works best with VR. Using that knowledge, we'll design and build our own elements for use in *Server 17*.

4
User Interface and User Experience inside VR

Thinking about our users and building our game systems with them in mind is just a small part of the overall process we need to go through to ensure that our game is an enjoyable experience for the widest range of players. **Human-Centered Design** (**HCD**) is just the first step in the greater design process called **User Experience** (**UX**) design. When we think about the whole user experience, we are really looking at not only the people who are using our game, but also at what we can do to improve how they use it. By thinking through the lens of UX, we hope to build a game that addresses all of the player's needs, is easy to use, and that the player never wants to put down.

In this chapter, we will cover the following topics:

- What is UX design?
- The seven aspects of UX
- User interfaces in VR
- Designing the UI for *Server 17*

What is UX design?

The term UX design is not a new term, even though its use has become more popular in recent years. Coined by Don Norman during his time at Apple, it is an umbrella term for the many ways in which people interact with machines. It also refers to the idea of seeing things from the user's perspective. In the game industry, UX tends to go hand in hand with user interface design since players often interact with a piece of software purely through its interface. Yet the development of virtual reality and its ability to give players a large amount of choice in how they interact with a game world has led companies to rethink how they view this field. How do you think about the user experience in a game when the player can interact with the world without a traditional UI? This is where the UX designer really comes into their own.

A UX designer is a designer who is responsible for the look, feel, and usability of the product. Yet, even this definition is lacking since, until recently, UX design in video games pretty much meant focusing on the user interface. In virtual reality development, UX design covers several more topics, such as story experience, control schemes, player safety, accessibility, and more. A UX designer should be concerned with seven different aspects of the game. The game needs to have the following characteristics:

- **Useful**: Does the game provide the user with the experience they are looking for? There is no reason to bring a game or product to market if it isn't useful to someone. In UX design, we use the Discovery and Empathy stages of HCD to discover how useful what we are designing will be for our users.
- **Usable**: Can the user achieve their objectives while using the product? A game cannot be successful if it is difficult to play or understand. There are many factors that contribute to a video game's usability, such as the controls, character animation, difficulty, and more.
- **Accessible**: Accessibility continues to be an important part of user experience design. Users with different ability levels should be able to play your game, and the experience you offer should be accessible to anyone. When we sit down and design for accessibility, we often find that we improve the experience for everyone. Several organizations have released developer resources to help bring more accessible games to market, such as `https://accessible.games/` and `http://gameaccessibilityguidelines.com/`.

- **Desirable**: Desirability refers to the marketing, branding, and aesthetic of a game or franchise. When we design for desirability, we want to create an image or emotional attachment that players want. The goal is to create a game experience that players will brag about and create a desire for that game in their friends.

- **Findable**: Findability refers to how easy a game is to find and purchase, but it also refers to how easy it is to find experiences contained within it the game. Imagine that a player purchases the latest arena shooter. They are excited to play with their friends, so they load the game, but can't seem to find the play button or the options to customize the controls. They search through countless menus that allow them to make a character and tweak the sound, but just can't get to the point where they can play with their buddies. Finally, they just give up and drop the controller. As developers, the last thing we want to is waste our players' time and cause them frustration. This is why findability is so important.

- **Valuable**: Players often find value based on factors such as online capabilities, hours of gameplay, announced features, and difficulty. The more value the player sees in the game, the more likely they are to purchase it. Terefore, the main goal of us designers is to have players see the value in our games and purchase them so that we can continue to design and create more experiences.

- **Credible**: This is the players' ability to trust the developer to deliver the experience and features they have been promised. Credibility is an important commodity in the game industry, and one that we have seen publishers/developers take for granted in recent years. We only have one chance for our game to make a good first impression, and most players never give a product a second chance. This is especially important for smaller independent developers who rely on reputation and word of mouth to sell their games.

Together, these seven aspects of game design create the basis for a way to think about the user experience. When we design games with our players' needs, goals, and overall experience in mind, we create products that are fun, memorable, and successful in the marketplace. With this idea in mind, let's move on to creating the next portion of *Server 17*: the user interface elements that will be critical for controlling the experience and for conveying necessary information to the player.

User interfaces in VR

As we have seen, interaction in VR goes beyond what we are used to in traditional applications and video games. The player has near total immersion in the game world and can reach out and touch many of the objects they wish to interact with. This ability to interact directly with the environment opens many avenues for interface design while also presenting several challenges. One such challenge is that HUD elements that are displayed along the edges of a screen appear distorted and out of position in VR. Such elements can also break the immersion of the VR experience, depending on the story and setting. To solve the interface problem, most VR developers have moved away from these interfaces in favor of using information elements embedded within the game world. These can be broken down into the following three categories:

- Diagetic
- Spatial
- Meta

Let's take a look at diagetic interfaces, as shown in the following screenshot:

The Server 17 level clock

Diagetic interface elements exist within the game world and provide the player with information directly from the environment. The map the player carries in *Minecraft* or *Firewatch*, the energy bars built into the suit of Isaac Clarke in *Dead Space*, and the watch that the player refers to in the *Metro* games are all examples of information being provided to the player by contextual clues inside the environment. Diagetic interfaces are preferred in virtual reality as they promote immersion and do not create any ill effects for the player.

Next up are spatial interfaces, as shown in the following screenshot:

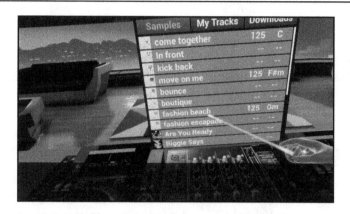

Spatial interface elements in Tribe XR

Sometimes the best way to provide information to the player is to have it floating right in front of their face. Spatial interface elements float at designated world coordinates in the game world, waiting for the player to read or interact with them. We see these interfaces in many current VR titles—for example, the song menu in *Beat Saber*, the track selection interface in *Tribe XR*, and the ammo counters in *Robo Recall*. Spatial interface elements perform well in virtual reality as they blend in with the virtual world and often mimic traditional UI elements that players are used to using.

Finally, we have meta interfaces:

Interface elements in *Robo Recall*

Meta interface elements are defined as two-dimensional elements that are displayed as an overlay on the player's vision, but that are not persistent like a standard interface. These are often used to convey temporary information, such as damage, without a more permanent presence on the screen. The most common use of this type of interface is a blood splatter or red tinted vision to display damage in games such as *Gorn* and *Robo Recall*.

Designing the UI elements for Server 17

Taking what we now know about user experience and interfaces, let's apply that knowledge to creating some UI elements for *Server 17*. For our first-time VR user, our interface elements should probably be diagetic for both ease of use and to preserve immersion in our Sci-Fi environment. We need to display our level timer so that the player knows how much time they have left. We also might need to rethink how the tools station is used to streamline the station interface. As always, remember to test with your user group along the way along the way and remember that you are designing the game to maximize their enjoyment!

Displaying the level timer

Let's start by designing the level timer, as shown in the following diagram:

Level timer wireframe created using a basic UI wireframe software

To keep the timer as simple as possible, we need to create something that is easily seen from anywhere in the level and does not take the player out of the experience. First, our timer should be digital to fit the Sci-Fi setting of our game. Second, it should be located in a place that the player finds natural to look at and can be easily found anywhere in the level. Finally, it should be able to display minutes and seconds, rather than just seconds, to fit the player's expectation of what a timer is. This is what I think would make a good solution.

Creating a diagetic timer element will preserve the Sci-Fi experience for the player, as well as create something that is easy to read. We can locate our widget above the puzzle itself and allow it to rotate to always face the player. This will meet all of our criteria and create something that is fun and fits with our theme.

Our timer solution will consist of two different parts. The first is an **Unreal Motion Graphics (UMG)** widget scripted to calculate the level time. The second piece will be a class blueprint that displays our 2D widget in our 3D level.

When preparing for this book, I was asked by several people to discuss the difference between 2D and 3D interface assets in VR. 2D interface elements work in virtual reality as long as they exist as spatial or diagetic components. 3D pieces, such as the button and tool station we developed in the last chapter, work as well, specifically because they are diagetic in nature. The most important consideration should always be your players and their expectations. Research and testing will always help you design the best solution.

We will start by creating the UMG widget, as shown in the following screenshot:

The UMG widget canvas

To create a UMG widget, go through the following steps:

1. Right-click in the **Content Browser**, mouse over the **User Interface** option, and select **Widget Blueprint**. Name the new widget `LevelTimer`. Double-click the new blueprint to open it.

2. Our design consists of two text components, one a label and one that is updated every frame to display the time. Create the first one by using the **Palette** panel to find the **Text** component and dragging it on to the **Canvas Panel**.

3. In the **Details** panel, change the name to `TraceLabel`.

4. In the **Slot** section of the **Details** panel, click the **Anchors** drop-down menu and choose the center option. This will keep it centered within our class blueprint.

5. Change the **Position X** value to **-150** and the **Position Y** value to **-125**.

6. Change the **Size X** value to **300** and the **Size Y** value to **100**.

7. In the **Appearance** section of the **Details** panel, change the color of the text to something bright. I went with a green color, but feel free to change it to whatever you might like.

8. In the **Font** portion of the **Appearance** section, change the **Size** value to **48**.

9. Finally, change the **Justification** option to **center**.

10. With our font option set, we can now update the text. In the **Content** section of the **Details** panel, change the **Text** value to `TRACE ACTIVE`.

11. Create the second **Text** component and name it `TimerDisplay`.

12. Just like before, click the **Anchors** drop-down menu and change it to the **center** option.

13. Change the **Position X** value to **-150** and the **Position Y** value to **-50**.

14. Change the **Size X** value to **300** and the **Size Y** value to **100**.

15. In the **Appearance** section of the **Details** panel, change the color to the same value that you used in step 7.

16. In the **Font** portion of the **Appearance** section, change the **Size** value to **48**.

17. Change the **Justification** to center.

18. In the content section of the panel, change the **Text** value to "**MM:SS**".

19. Now we need to program the **Text** value to update and display the time remaining in our level. To do this we will create a bit of programming called a **Bind**. Click the **Bind** drop-down list to the right of the **Text** value and choose **Create Binding**, as shown in the following screenshot:

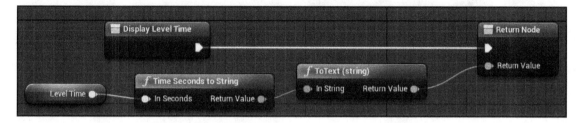

Display Level Time binding

20. Let's start with a bit of housekeeping. In the **Functions** section of the **My Blueprint** panel, right-click on the name of our binding and choose the **Rename** option. Change the name to **Display Level Time**.

21. This binding needs to be able to take the level time that is measured in seconds, convert it to minutes and seconds, and then display it as a string. The first step will be to create a new float variable that will hold our level time. Over in the **Variables** section of the **My Blueprint** panel, create a new float variable and name it **Level Time**.

22. Drag a copy of our new variable into the blueprint, and choose **Get** from the menu. From here, we will delve a bit into Unreal's timespan system. We will use a node called **Time Seconds to String** to convert our seconds that are stored in **Level Time** to a string that is in the m*inutes:seconds:milliseconds* format. From there, we can convert the new string into text and feed it into our text component. Right-click and search for the **Time Seconds to String** node and connect **Level Time** to the **In Seconds** input.

23. From there, plug the output from **Time Seconds to String** into the **Return** input and Unreal will create the translate node for us, as shown in the following screenshot:

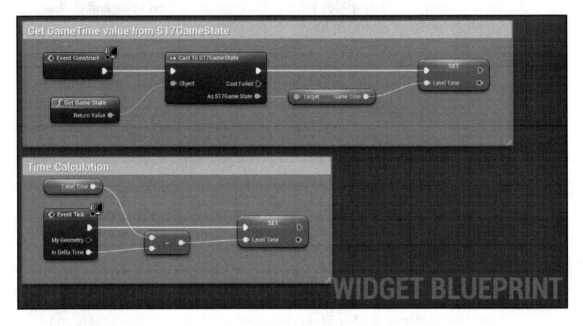

Event graph for level timer widget

24. Now to finish the setup for our timer. We will need to cast to S17GameState to retrieve the value of **GameTime** and that as our value for the **Level Time**. This allows us to change the value in one place and have it affect the timer automatically. Click over to the **Event Graph** for our widget and drag an execute line off the **Event Construct** node. Search for **Cast To S17GameState**.

25. Let's set up the cast. Drag a connection from the **Object** input, and search for the **Get Game State** node. With this defined, we can now pretend to be the **Game State** and retrieve the value of **GameTime**. Drag a connection from the S17GameState output and search for the **Get Game Time** node.

26. Lastly, we need to store the value of **GameTime** inside our **Level Time** node. Drag a copy of the **Level Time** variable into the blueprint and choose the set option, **Connect** this to the execute output from our cast node and connect the output from getting the value of **GameTime** into the float input for **Level Time**.

27. To finally make our timer work, every tick we will quickly calculate the new time for **Level Time**. Combined with our **Bind** function, this will display the current remaining level time in our widget. Grab a copy of the **Level Time** variable and drag it into our blueprint. Choose **Get** from the menu and position it near the **Event Tick** node.

28. Drag another copy of the **Level Time** into the blueprint, only this time, choose **Set** from the menu. Connect this to the execute output from **Event Tick**.

29. Math time! We will use the **In Delta Seconds** output from **Event Tick** to calculate the time remaining in the level by subtracting it from the current value of **Level Time**. Drag a line off from the get **Level Time** node and search for `Float-Float`. Make sure the first value in this new node is **Level Time** and connect the **In Delta Second** output to the second input. Connect the output of this node to the float input on the set **Level Time**.

With our timer functionality all set up, all that remains to do is display it in the level. To do this, we will make use of a class blueprint that contains a `Widget` component. This component allows us to display a 2D interface element in 3D space by projecting the widget on-to a plane. We can then position this plane over the puzzle and program it to always rotate to face the player. In this way, we can guarantee that the player can always see our countdown clock.

Start by creating a new **Class Blueprint** extended from **Actor** and name it `3dLevelTimer`:

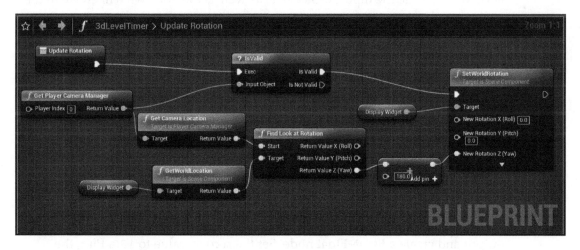

3dLevelTimer function

Let's add the **Widget** component by going through the following steps:

1. In the **Viewport** section of our blueprint, click the **Add Component** button and search for the **Widget** component. Add it to the blueprint and name it **Display Widget**.

2. Click on the new **Display Widget** in the **Components** panel. In the **Details** panel, find the **Widget Class** option in the **User Interface** section of the menu. Click the drop-down menu and select the **Level Timer** widget we created earlier.

3. Next, we will create a new function to handle the rotation of the widget. In the **Functions** section of the **My Blueprints** panel, click the + function button. Name the new function **Update Rotation**.

4. The purpose of the **Update Rotation** function is to find the location of the player's camera and rotate the widget around to face it so that our player can always look and see how much time is left. Start the function by dragging a line from the start node and searching for the **IsValid** node. We only want the widget to worry about rotating if the player is in the level.

5. From **IsValid**, drag a line from the **IsValid** output, and search for the **SetWorldRotation** node that references the **Display Widget**. Right-click on the **New Rotation** input and split the struct pin. We will need this for later.

6. Going back to the **IsValid** node, we still need to find the **Input Object**. Drag a line off the input, and search for the **Get Player Camera Manager** node. This node will provide the input for **IsValid**, as well as the node we will create in the next step.

7. Dragging another connection from the **Get Player Camera Manager** node, search for **Get Camera Location**. This will be the start location for finding our look at rotation.

8. From the **Return Value** of **Get Camera Location**, drag a line and create a **Find Look At Rotation** node. To get the **Target** for our new node, we will need to drag a reference to our **Display Widget** into the blueprint from the **Components** panel. From this, create a **Get World Location** node and connect its output to the **Target** input on **Find Look At Rotation**.

9. Almost there! Right-click on the **Return Value** pin from the **Find Look At Rotation** node and split the struct. We only need to work with the **Yaw** value. If we work with the **Yaw** as it is, our widget will be rotated backwards. We can correct this with a little bit of math. Drag a connection from the **Return Value Z** output and create a **Float+Float** node. Set the second value to 180. Plug the output into the **New Rotation Z** input on the **Set World Rotation** node.

10. Time to add the new function to the **Event Graph**. Drag a copy of the **UpdateRotation** function into the blueprint and connect it to a copy of the **Event Tick** node. We are ready to test!

Programming complete! Drag a copy of the `3dLevelTimer` into your test level, and position it above the puzzle. Now test the new feature on yourself, as well as on your potential users. Pay attention to their feedback and adjust the size, color, and location of the timer as needed.

Redesigning the tool experience

Having applied user experience design principles to our level timer, let's go back and take a look at the **Tools Station** we created in the last chapter. When testing with my users, I discovered that it was not intuitive for the player to have to head for a tool station every time they wanted to rotate the puzzle, especially within a timed experience. When we receive feedback like this, there is only one solution: redesign! Let's look at the following diagram:

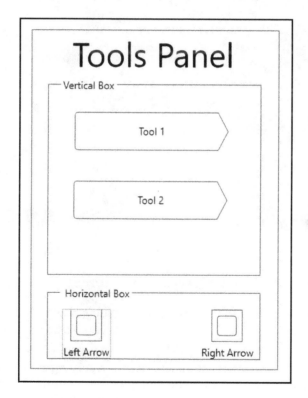

New tools menu wireframe

After a couple of rounds of testing and interviews with my players, it became clear that having to go back to the tool station to rotate the puzzle (and use other future tools) was adding a step where there didn't need to be one. The tool station itself was a neat idea, but it didn't bring any additional value to the game experience. In fact, it made the experience less usable. The new goal will be to redesign the station as a tool menu that will be connected to the player's controller. This menu could be opened at any time or location and used in the same manner as the tool station, without having to move.

It will need to be built in two parts, similar to the level timer. The first will be a 2D widget that will contain all the functionality. The second will be a 3D widget that we can display whenever a button on the controller is pressed. We can see this setup in the following screenshot:

The completed ToolsWidget interface

Start by creating a new blueprint widget and naming it `ToolsWidget`:

1. Right-click in the **Content Browser** and create a new blueprint widget named `ToolsWidget`. Double-click the blueprint to open the UMG editor.

2. This time when we make our widget, we are going to take a more organized approach. Start by searching the **Palette** for the **Image** component. Drag it on to the **Canvas Panel** and change the **Anchors** option in the **Details** panel to the center. Change its name to `Background`. This will give our menu a nice background color.

3. Change the **Position X** and **Position Y** values to -62.5.

4. Change the **Size X** and **Size Y** values to 125.

5. Time to choose the color. Choose your new color with the **Color** and **Opacity** option. Setting your **Alpha** value to 0.5 gives it a nice Sci-Fi technology feel.

6. Now we are going to create a **Vertical Box** component and add it to the **Canvas** panel. Don't forget to change its **Anchors** option to center.

7. Like the **Background**, change the **Position X** and **Position Y** values to -62.5, as well as the **Size X** and **Size Y** values to 125.

8. The **Vertical Box** organizes every component we place in it equally throughout the vertical space. We will use this to keep our buttons perfectly distributed in the menu. Start by dragging a **Text** component into the **Vertical Box**. Change the **Horizontal Alignment** to center and the **Font Size** to 14. Set the **Text** to say **Tools Menu**.

9. Now we are going to add a few buttons. Two will be used to rotate the puzzle left and right. We will also build two buttons that can be used to program additional tools in the future. **Head** to the **Palette** and search for the **Button** component. Drag two copies into the **Vertical Box**. In the **Details** panel, change the **Padding** value of both buttons to 5.

10. Name the first button Tools1_BTN and the second button Tools2_BTN.

11. Each button now needs a text label. Use the **Palette** to find the **Text** component and drag one on to each of our buttons. For each one, change the **Font Size** to 10. Change the **Text** to **Tool 1** and **Tool 2**.

12. Now we will use a **Horizontal Box** to organize our rotation buttons. Use the search box in the **Palette** panel to find the **Horizontal Box** and drag a copy into our **Vertical Box**. In the **Details** panel, set the **Size** option to **Fill**.

13. Drag two copies of the **Button** component into the **Horizontal Box**. Name the first button Left_BTN and the second Right_BTN. Set the **Padding** to 5 and **Size** option to **Fill**.

14. Add a label to each button. Drag a **Text** component on to the left button. Set the **Font Size** to 10 and change the **Text** value to <---.

15. Do the same for the right button, but set the Text value to --->.

We now have a nice basic interface that is ready to be programmed. The plan is to program the left and right puzzle rotation buttons in a similar fashion to the tool station we created earlier. The additional tool buttons that we created will be left without functionality for the time being. Time to take a look at the code, as shown in the following screenshot:

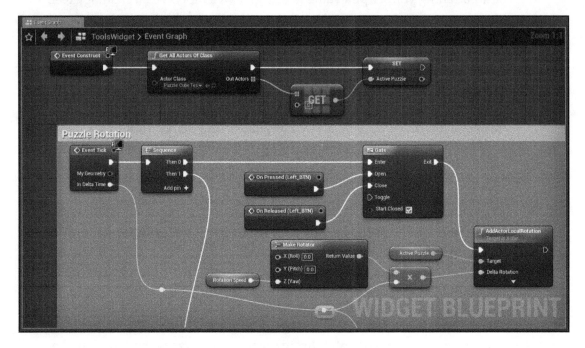

ToolsWidget programming blueprint

To be able to rotate our puzzle, we first need to find a reference to it by going through the following steps:

1. We need to be able to find the puzzle that is in our level as soon as the interface is created. To do this, we will use the **Event Construct** node. Head over to the **Graph,** and create one using the **Palette** panel, if there isn't one already there.
2. To find the puzzle, we are going to use a node called **Get All Actors of Class**. This node is able to find every copy of a specific class inside your level and dump it into a temporary array. Drag an execute line from **Event Construct** and drop it. Search for **Get All Actors of Class,** and set the **Actor Class** option to **PuzzleCubeTest**.

3. The **Out Actors** output gives us an array containing any instances of **PuzzleCubeTest**. In this case, there is only one. To access it, we will use the **Get** (a copy) node. Drag a line from the **Out Actors** output, and create one using the menu. The node will access index 0, the first slot in the array, which should contain our one and only reference to **PuzzleCubeTest**.

4. Drag a line from the output of the **Get** node and choose **Promote to Variable** from the menu. This will place our puzzle reference in a variable we can use. Name the new variable **ActivePuzzle**. Connect the execute output from the event to the **Set** node that was created for our new variable.

5. With our puzzle reference in place, it is now time to create the rotation. Just like when we created our 3D button, we will use the **In Delta Time** output from the node to control our rotation. Create an **Event Tick** node if there is not one already in the blueprint.

6. Since we have to check for a button press for both the left and right button, we will need to use a **Sequence** node. Drag a line from the execute output of the **Event Tick** node, and create the **Sequence** node.

7. The **Then 0** branch will handle the **Left** button, and we will use the same technique we used when we created the original rotation code. Drag a line off the **Then 0** output, and create a **Gate** node.

8. Now we need a pressed and a released event to control the opening and closing of the gate. Head over to the **Variables** section of the **My Blueprints** panel and click on **Left_BTN**. Scroll to the bottom of the **Details** panel and click the + button next to the **On Pressed** and **On Released** options. Connect the **On Pressed** event to the **Open** input on the gate. Finally, connect the **On Released** event to the **Close** input.

9. We need to program the actual rotation using the **AddActorLocalRotation** node. Drag a line from the **Exit** output of the gate, and create the node. For the **Target**, head over to the **Variables** section and grab the **Active Puzzle** variable. Bring it into the blueprint and select **Get** from the menu. Plug it into the **Target** input on **AddActorLocalRotation**.

10. To get our **Delta Rotation,** we will multiply the change in time by a rotation speed. Create a new **Float** variable and name it **Rotation Speed**. Bring it into the blueprint and choose the **Get** option. Drag a line from its output, and create a **Make Rotator** node. Lastly, move the connection from the X input to the Z input.

11. Drag from the output of **Make Rotator** and connect a **Scale Rotator** node. This node takes a rotator and multiplies it by a float value. Connect the float input to the **In Delta Seconds** output from **Event Tick**.

12. Finally, connect the output of the **Scale Rotator** to the **Delta Rotation** input for **AddActorLocalRotation**, as shown in the following screenshot:

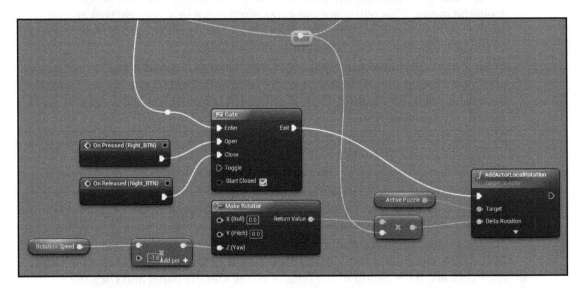

ToolsWidget puzzle rotation code

13. Repeat the steps from step 7 to step 12 for the **Then 1** branch to program the right button, but this time add a `Float * Float` node between the **Rotation Speed** and the **Make Rotator** node. Set the second value to **-1** to change the direction of the rotation.

With the tools widget built and programmed, it's time to build the 3D widget to display it inside the level. We are going to use the same process we used to display the timer widget in the level, but this time, we will attach the 3D widget to the motion controller to give the feel of a wrist-mounted display, as shown in the following screenshot:

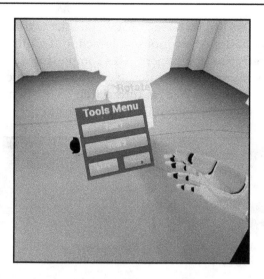

The ToolsWidget in action, mounted to the player's wrist

Right-click in the **Content Browser** and create a new **Class Blueprint** based on the **Actor**. Name it `3dToolsWidget`, double-click to open it, then go through the following steps:

1. In the **Components** panel, use the **Add Component** button to add a **Widget** component to the **Viewport**.

2. In the **Details** panel, rename this to `ToolsWidget`.

3. In the **User Interface** section of **Details**, click on the **Widget Class** drop-down menu, and choose our `ToolsWidget` interface.

4. Set the **X** and **Y** values for the **Draw Size** to `125`.

5. Time to add the interface to our `Server17PlayerPawn`. Find the player pawn in the **Content Browser** and double-click it to open it.

6. Let's add the interface to the motion controller. Click the **Add Component** button and search for the **Child Actor** component. Name it `ChildActor_ToolsWidget` and make it a child of `MotionController_L` in the hierarchy.

7. In the **Details** panel, set the **Child Actor Class** option to `3dToolsWidget`.

8. In the **Viewport**, use the move and rotate tools to position the widget at the left wrist, similar to a wristwatch. If you prefer to type the values in yourself, set the location values to *X=5*, *Y=-5*, and *Z=0*. For the rotation values, use *X=180*, *Y=0*, and *Z=-90*.

9. Since our interface display is quite large on the player's wrist, change the **Scale** values to *0.2*.

By default, motion controllers do not have a way to interact with 2D interface elements since they were originally designed for mouse interaction. To add this functionality, we need to use a **Widget Interaction** component. This component was designed by Epic Games to be the bridge between VR controllers and traditional interfaces, and just takes a little setup to use. Start by adding a **Widget Interaction** component to the Server17PlayerPawn, as shown in the following screenshot:

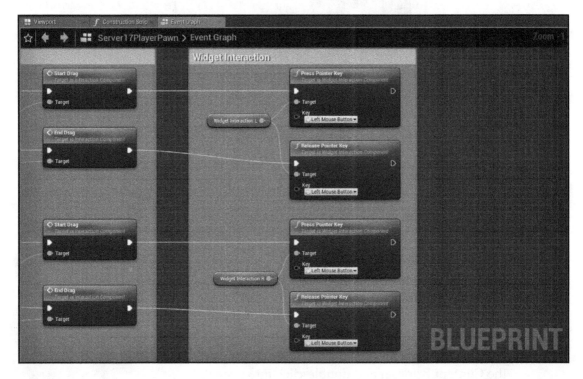

Widget Interaction component

We will add one of these components to each motion controller:

1. In the **Components** panel, use the **Add Component** button to add two copies of the **Widget Interaction** component. Make one a child of **MotionController_L** and name it **Widget Interaction L**. Make the other a child of **MotionController_R** and name it **Widget Interaction R**. This will give the functionality to both hands.

2. The **Widget Interaction** component allows us to simulate a mouse pointer. We can also simulate a mouse click with just a little bit of code. Head over to the Event Graph for our player pawn and locate our trigger code. We can add the functionality on the end of the existing sequence. Drag an execute line from from the end of the left trigger sequence, drop it, and search for the **Press Pointer Key** (**Widget Interaction L**) node. Use the Key drop-down list to choose the **Left Mouse Button**.

3. Drag a line from the output from the reference to **Widget Interaction L** that we just created, and search for the **Release Pointer** key node. Set the **Key** drop-down menu to **Left Mouse Button,** and connect an execute line back to the **End Drag** node.

4. Repeat the process for **Widget Interaction R** to give the same functionality to our right trigger.

At this point, we can test our interface. Make sure that the rotate functionality is working and that the position at the left wrist is correct. There is one more bit of programming to do to finish this menu. Let's make it so that the menu can be toggled on and off using the menu button on the motion controller. This way, a player can hide it if they are not using it. To do this, we will need to use the **MotionController (L) Shoulder** event, as shown in the following screenshot:

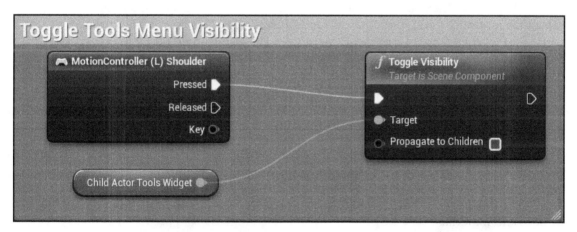

ToolsWidget toggle code

Start by creating the event node by going through the following steps:

1. Right-click in the **Event Graph** for `Server17PlayerPawn`, and search for the **MotionController (L) Shoulder** event. Create it and position it near the rest of our button code.
2. Drag an execution line from the **Pressed** output and drop it. Search for the **Toggle Visibility (ChildActor_ToolsWidget)** and place it in the blueprint.
3. Go back to the **Viewport** for our player pawn, and click on the **ChildActor_ToolsWidget**. In the **Details** panel, turn off the **Visibility** option.

And done! We have now constructed two different interface elements that make more use of 2D menu components, and we have learned how to display them in a 3D space. We have programmed them to interact with the world and added the ability to simulate mouse interaction to our motion controllers so that we can use them. Just think of all the great interactive menus you could now create for your virtual reality experiences, using either 3D objects or 2D interfaces!

Summary

In this chapter, we learned about user experience and how HCD is just one small part of this much larger field. We explored the field of UX design and how VR has caused it to expand beyond traditional interface interactions. We also learned about the seven aspects of user experience that are important. From there, we took a look at the different types of user interfaces and learned what works best in virtual reality. Finally, we applied our new knowledge of user experience and VR-ready interfaces to design and create the interface widgets for our level.

In the next chapter, we will discuss how to create eye-popping visual elements for virtual reality games. Like gameplay elements and user interfaces, art for VR games has different requirements than art created for traditional video games. Optimization is key to keeping performance high and our player comfortable. We will look at some techniques for creating our lighting and visual effects, as well as what is needed to make the most of our static meshes and materials.

5
Creating Optimized Game Art for VR in UE4

Server 17 has come a long way. We have brought the game from a simple puzzle idea to a working game prototype. At this stage, we have a sample level, custom gameplay, and custom interfaces. We have built interaction systems that can be expanded to add even more game mechanics. However, the game is not much to look at, is it? Our lighting is basic. We are still using the default textures for many things. There is nothing wrong with it, since this is still a game prototype, but if we want to be able to present this to anyone beyond family and friends, it is going to need a bit of sprucing up.

Creating 3D game art for VR is not like creating game art for other titles. Though we use many of the same programs, VR requires us to be conservative with our art. The performance requirements of VR demand that we keep polygon counts low, use tricks to eliminate the use of advanced lighting techniques, and rethink our approach to art. Fake everything you can, and treat your game art as if it is the late, 90s.

In this chapter, we will cover the following topics:

- Performance is key
- Artistic limitations in VR
- Performance-boosting techniques
- Measuring ingame performance

Performance is key

Again and again, we have touched on the theme of performance in VR. We talked about it first when we discussed VR sickness in `Chapter 1`, *Introducing VR Technology in Unreal Engine 4*. We touched on it again in `Chapter 3`, *Exploring Riveting Gameplay in Virtual Reality*, when we programmed the interaction systems that make our game work. So, why do we keep talking about it? Performance is central to enjoying a VR experience. Having high-end visuals helps our players become immersed in our digital environments, while keeping steady frame rates is the best way to maximize player comfort and reduce VR sickness. So, how do we balance both of these needs?

In this chapter, we are going to talk about performance regarding to 3D game art, lighting, and visual effects. In VR, managing your assets and detail level becomes a balancing act. How do we provide the visuals required to engage our players while keeping framerates at 90 FPS or above to keep them comfortable? The simple answer is understanding and careful planning. With the right planning and a few tricks, we can keep our FPS high, and deliver the experience our players demand.

To start us off, let's discuss the important points of how VR renders the elements we place on the screen. Each object we create and add to our environment needs to go through the process of being drawn to the screen. The more detailed the object (as measured by the polygon count or the triangle count), the more processing it takes. Processing takes time. We also have to be aware of draw calls. Each time we update the screen, the object needs to be drawn again along with each material that it uses. We could describe this as follows:

*Draw Calls = Number of Meshes on screen * Number of Materials per Mesh*

We also have to remember that VR headsets render to two screens (one per eye). So the number of draw calls is actually doubled! This is where planning can help. Here are some helpful do's and don'ts:

- **Do's:**
  - Plan our environment so we can minimize the number of meshes on the screen. Make sure that each mesh has a purpose and adds something to the level by being there.
  - Minimize the number of materials that are on each object. It is possible to create one large material that can be used with several different meshes. However, keeping the number of materials per object as low as possible works as well.

- **Don'ts**:
  - Place meshes just to fill space. This makes the level feel cluttered and busy. This also increases the number of draw calls per frame.
  - Depend on advanced rendering techniques to display meshes and effects. Features such as transparency, screen-space reflections, and normal maps do not work well in VR. Either they are too resource intensive or do not display correctly.

These are just a couple of the ways knowledge and planning can help with performance. By understanding the demands of VR and planning our approach to the art, we can do our best to minimize draw calls.

Artistic limitations in VR

Now that we have a basic understanding, it's time to get specific. How do the limitations we face in VR affect each of the following categories of game art?:

- Static and skeletal meshes
- Materials
- Lighting
- Visual effects

Each category represents different limitations that need to be considered when creating the visuals for our game.

Static and skeletal mesh limitations

Let's start by taking a look at static and skeletal meshes:

The static mesh editor in Unreal 4

Static and skeletal meshes represent the majority of the art that goes into creating a game in Unreal Engine 4. These are your 3D models and tend to be sorted into groups such as environment, character, weapon, vehicle, and so on. Back in the late '90s when computer resources were more limited, artists had to work within strict limits when it came to polygon or triangle counts, but those limits are a thing of the past. Modern game hardware can push millions of triangles to the screen with no problems. However, with the performance needs of VR being so high, it is time to create our models like it's 1999!

For some of us older folks, we are able to remember what those limitations were like. For others of us (younger readers), we need a bit of a refresher on what that means. Today's standards for triangle counts are quite high. A first-person weapon can be 30,000 triangles or more. It is not uncommon for characters to have a triangle count of up to 120,000 triangles. However, every bit of extra detail can impact performance. Without normal maps to help us fake detail and decrease these numbers, how can we maintain the level of detail that we need for a high-end environment? A common practice is to delete the polygons on objects in places that the player won't see. How can we do that when the player can see all around our objects?

Material limitations

Next, let's discuss materials:

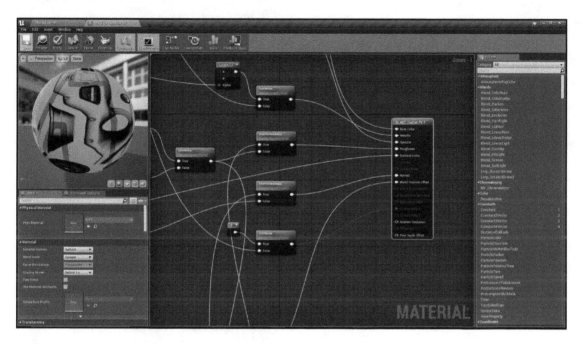

A glimpse of the material editor

The complexity and number of a scene's materials is often the major reason for poor performance in VR. Each material that we apply to a mesh adds a draw call to our game, forcing the computer to work harder each frame. This can result in slower performance and not being able to hit our 90 FPS target. There is also the issue of transparency and reflections. Transparent and translucent materials are a fantastic effect. However, they are costly in VR, as the material has to be reevaluated and redrawn every frame. Reflections are another great effect that helps a world feel more realistic and immersive. Yet, these are also very resource intensive and require complex calculations.

Lighting limitations

It's now time to look at lighting:

An example of lighting in UE4

Many modern games make use of dynamic light sources to provide players with a living world. Shadows move as the sun marches across the sky. NPCs cast shadows as they move under street lamps. This type of lighting and shadow help us feel grounded in the world and are an essential part of any game. However, dynamic lighting is very expensive to calculate for every frame. So, how can we use shadows to keep the realism in our virtual worlds?

Visual Effects (VFX) limitations

Lastly, we come to visual effects:

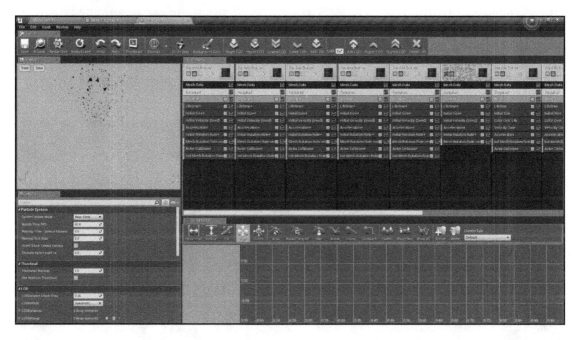

Unreal Engine 4 Cascade VFX editor

The right visual effects bring a punch and excitement to many different kinds of games. They are essential in action games. They bring a sense of impact to sports games. They even add to the realism and feel of simulations. Yet, much like dynamic lighting, they are costly when it comes to performance. The limitations on translucent and transparent materials apply here. Making some techniques such as the use of SubUV textures (laying out the frames of an animated particle in a grid) ineffective. Many particles also contain dynamic light sources.

Performance-boosting techniques

With the player's comfort to consider and all of these limitations, how are designers creating amazing 3D worlds for VR users to step into? The answer can be summed up in the phase *fake it till you make it*. The technology behind VR is rapidly evolving. New techniques for dealing with the issues we've mentioned are being built into the next generation of game engines. However, for now, there are some best practices currently being used by artists in the industry today to deliver amazing visuals, such as the showdown demo from Epic Games:

The showdown demo from Epic Games

These guys were able to render this amazing scene at 90 FPS. There is transparency, lighting, and visual effects. The models used are from various other UE4 demos and are not reduced in quality. Here is just some of how they did it.

Static and skeletal mesh techniques

The best way to maximize the success of your VR environment in terms of performance is to approach the scene with a plan and be as conservative as possible. Since the player has the opportunity to scrutinize and interact with the environment more than in a traditional game, VR-ready assets need to be scaled for users of an average height. Meshes must also be manifold. This means ensuring that the object is complete and there are no missing polygons in the mesh, since the player can usually view the object from any angle. Here is an example of a DJ deck that was created for *Tribe XR*:

Pioneer CDJ used in Tribe XR open in Autodesk Maya. This mesh is only 2,001 triangles

In their game *Tribe XR*, the team planned and focused their VR DJing experience to fit in one room so that they could maximize the ability to create an immersive Sci-Fi environment. Inspired by games such as *Overwatch* and *Team Fortress 2*, the lounge they have created has just enough meshes in it to give it that lived-in feel. Each one is placed with purpose to create a relaxed and believable atmosphere. The meshes they used have low polygon/triangle counts, and UV maps are optimized to reduce redundant draw calls. The result is a smooth VR experience that keeps framerates high and players absorbed in the music.

 Standard methods of game optimization, such as the use of **Level of Detail** (**LOD**) meshes, is still viable in VR and should still be considered.

Material techniques

As mentioned previously, materials for VR should be planned and designed to minimize the number of draw calls that are required in every frame. Each mesh should incorporate the minimum number of materials to reduce these draw calls. In the showdown demo, Epic Games created many purpose-built props, though some were taken from previous demos, such as the Samaritan demo. The meshes constructed for VR all follow a similar pattern. All are optimized with low triangle counts, and most utilize only one material.

The translucency/transparency is kept to a minimum and only used in a handful of locations, such as the glass in vehicles. The glass in the surrounding buildings has been faked through the texture images that are used. In places where translucency is needed, the **DitherTemporalAA** material node can be used to make opacity-masked objects look like translucent ones. Here is one example using a rocket smoke trail:

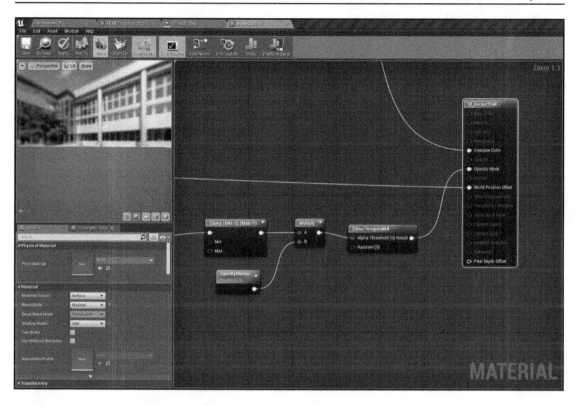

The RocketTrail material from the showdown demo

Specifically, using the **DitherTemporalAA** node helps eliminate pixel overdraw, and this improves performance.

Finally, we have a powerful tool in helping us fine-tune the materials in our scenes: the **Shader Complexity** view. Accessed through the **View Mode** drop-down menu in the viewport, this view shades the scene in greens and reds, with green being less complex and red being more complex. Let's look at this screenshot from the showdown demo:

The showdown demo with Shader Complexity enabled

Most of the scene is overlayed in green, showing us that there is a minimum number of shader instructions for most objects in the level. Where we see red is the transparent windshield glass and the shaders used on the characters that were taken from the infiltrator demo (these are not optimized for VR).

Lighting techniques

Lighting a level is one of the most resource intensive processes that happens every frame update. When dynamic lights move, it changes shadows, reflections, and scattered light, which all have to be recalculated and redrawn. To compensate for this, Unreal Engine 4 gives the option to bake lightmaps for each object. This creates static lighting by baking the lighting data into a lightmap on each object. Lightmaps can't be as realistic as dynamic lighting, but the performance difference is very dramatic. That isn't to say that dynamic lighting doesn't have a place in VR projects. Dynamic lights may still be used in limited numbers, and they should never touch one another. If the scene you are creating is an outdoor scene, try setting your directional light (sun or moon) to dynamic, and then use cascading shadow maps with the simplest settings you can.

However, the problem with using static lighting is the loss of shadows for your dynamic objects. Things such as the player, enemies, and interactive objects just seem to float within your virtual space, without a shadow to ground them. This gives the space a somewhat-unnatural look. To fix this, we can use a technique that can create a fake blob shadow. We can see it here in the showdown demo:

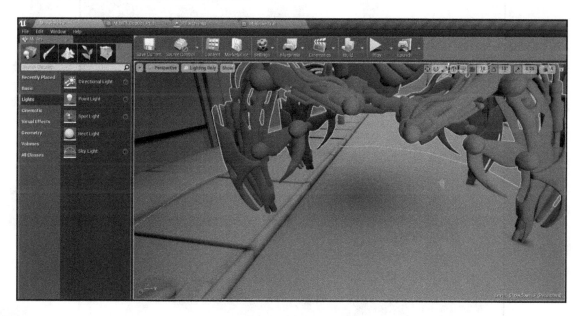

A static mesh with a fake blob shadow

Finally, reflections can go a long way to giving an area a feeling of complexity and realism. However, real-time reflections use a significant amount of resources and are not well-suited to VR games. In the spirit of *fake it till you make it,* the designers at Epic Games created the reflection-capture actor. These actors grab reflections from within their areas of influence and encode them into static cube maps. These cube maps can then be used by materials to create and fine-tune reflections in the level. Since these cube maps are created before the game begins, they have very little impact on the level of performance.

Visual effects techniques

If you've done much game development work, whether it is two or three dimensional, then you are aware of the traditional SubUV technique for creating particle effects. This technique involves creating a sprite sheet that represents a particle, such as fire or smoke, and having the game engine animate through the cells. This creates an animated particle that looks three dimensional but is actually a 2D texture. Here is an example of smoke:

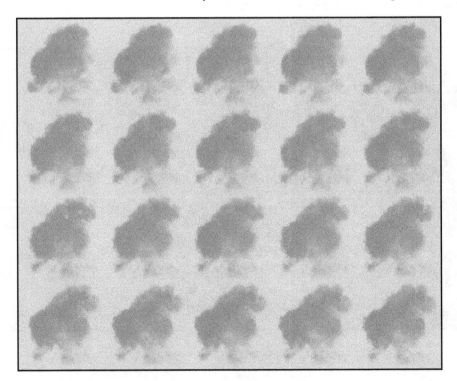

Smoke particle created with the SubUV technique

Your first thought might be that this type of particle would be ideal for VR since we are projecting a smoke particle with a 2D texture. However, since the technique depends on transparency, creating this particle in VR would be tough on our performance. We would also need to consider that players in VR can view the particles from many different angles. Because of this, particles created using the SubUV technique end up looking flat and uninteresting. Designers can work around these issues by focusing on using small meshes as particles and creating effects that are close to the camera:

A VR-friendly particle open in Cascade

In the showdown demo, smoke is used at several points in the level, such as part of the vehicle explosion that flips the car. To minimize the impact on performance, the designers created an animated smoke material that they were able to place on to a 3D ribbon mesh, which is then emitted along with several different types of concrete chunks as part of the effect. When the demo is viewed with the **Shader Complexity** view enabled, these smoke effects are shown with a green tint, meaning that they are optimized and have little impact on the framerate. This also allowed the designers to deploy these effects near or directly in front of the camera—something that can be done well with SubUV particles.

Measuring ingame performance

Over and over again, I have mentioned-performance as the most important consideration for a VR game. Yet, we have not talked about how to measure performance inside Unreal Engine 4 so that we can know whether we are optimizing well or not. Let's take a look at the tools we have available.

UE4 has an amazing number of performance profiling tools available as part of the game engine, more than I could discuss in this one-quick-start guide. However, I do want to discuss a couple that are relevant to our discussion: the **Stat** commands and the GPU Visualizer:

Scene Rendering [STATGROUP_scenerendering] Cycle counters (flat)	CallCount	InclusiveAvg	InclusiveMax	ExclusiveAvg	ExclusiveMax
RenderViewFamily		1.40 ms	2.10 ms	0.06 ms	0.15 ms
InitViews	1	0.37 ms	0.53 ms	0.01 ms	0.02 ms
FinishRenderViewTarget	1	0.36 ms	0.48 ms	0.00 ms	0.00 ms
Base pass drawing	1	0.14 ms	0.26 ms	0.01 ms	0.03 ms
StaticDrawList drawing	1	0.12 ms	0.24 ms	0.11 ms	0.22 ms
Depth drawing	1	0.10 ms	0.17 ms	0.09 ms	0.16 ms
DeferredShadingSceneRenderer Lighting	1	0.04 ms	0.55 ms	0.03 ms	0.53 ms
InitViewsPossiblyAfterPrepass	1	0.03 ms	0.04 ms	0.01 ms	0.01 ms
Translucency drawing	1	0.04 ms	0.08 ms	0.03 ms	0.07 ms
BeginOcclusionTests	1	0.04 ms	0.03 ms	0.04 ms	0.03 ms
RenderQuery Result					
Lighting drawing	1	0.01 ms	0.01 ms	0.00 ms	0.00 ms
DeferredShadingSceneRenderer Render Init	1	0.03 ms	0.06 ms	0.03 ms	0.06 ms
Proj Shadow drawing					
Dynamic shadow setup	1	0.01 ms	0.01 ms	0.00 ms	0.01 ms
Dynamic Primitive drawing	1	0.01 ms	0.02 ms	0.01 ms	0.02 ms
Cache Uniform Expressions	6	0.01 ms	0.04 ms	0.01 ms	0.04 ms
...ferredShadingSceneRenderer AfterBasePass	1	0.01 ms	0.02 ms	0.00 ms	0.02 ms
...gSceneRenderer FXSystem PostRenderOpaque	1	0.01 ms	0.02 ms	0.00 ms	0.02 ms
DeferredShadingSceneRenderer DBuffer	1	0.01 ms	0.01 ms	0.01 ms	0.01 ms
...dingSceneRenderer SetAndClearViewGBuffer	1	0.01 ms	0.07 ms	0.01 ms	0.07 ms
...dShadingSceneRenderer FXSystem PreRender	1	0.01 ms	0.01 ms	0.00 ms	0.01 ms
...ngSceneRenderer Render ServiceLocalQueue	23	0.01 ms	0.02 ms	0.01 ms	0.02 ms
...ShadingSceneRenderer AllocGBufferTargets	1	0.00 ms	0.01 ms	0.00 ms	0.01 ms
...eferredShadingSceneRenderer RenderFinish	1	0.00 ms	0.00 ms	0.00 ms	0.00 ms
[11 more stats. Use the stats.MaxPerGroup CVar to increase the limit]					

Counters	Average	Max
Present time	1.37 ms	2.67 ms
Mesh draw calls	77.00	77.00
Static list draw calls	70.00	70.00
Lights in scene		23.00
Translucency GPU Time (MS)	0.00	0.01

Stat command statistics

There are several Stat commands that can be useful for us to determine our performance. They are accessed by opening **Accessing the console** with the tilde key and typing in the following commands (they are not case-sensitive):

- **Stat FPS**: This command brings up the current framerate and the time it takes to render a frame in milliseconds. Remember that our target goal for HTC Vive and Oculus Rift is 90 FPS.
- **Stat Unit**: Displays in milliseconds the time per frame spent on rendering the frame, game calculations, draw calls, and GPU calculation time.
- **Stat SceneRendering**: Displays general render time statistics. When performance starts to drop, this panel can show us the culprit.

These statistics can help us understand whether our game is CPU bound or GPU bound. Being CPU bound means that our game has too many complex calculations and performance is currently being bottlenecked by the CPU. When our game is GPU bound, it means that we have too many draw calls, lights, or complex visuals, and our performance is being constrained by the graphics processor.

> Another simple method of determining whether we are CPU or GPU bound is to lower the graphics quality of the game and take a look at the effects on our framerate. If there is no change to the current FPS, then we are bound to the CPU.

The other tool we have is the GPU Visualizer:

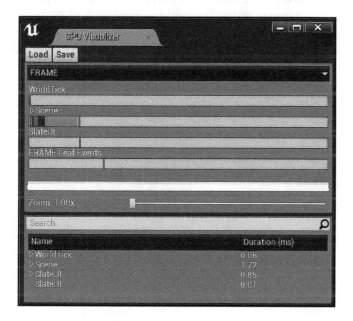

The GPU Visualizer

This is a visual interface that allows us to see the GPU cost of the render passes used to draw each frame. Though it may look complicated at first, this interface can show us which visual element or feature is causing the largest drop in performance, as indicated by the feature taking the largest number of milliseconds to render. With that knowledge, we can optimize the specific feature or remove it entirely. For more information on this subject, please refer to the *Performance and Profiling* section of the Unreal Engine 4 documentation located at https://docs.unrealengine.com/en-us/Engine/Performance.

Summary

In this chapter, we learned several of the known causes of performance issues in VR games related to static and skeletal meshes, materials, lighting, and visual effects. After discussing the causes, we explored several different solutions using some examples from the DJ simulation *Tribe XR* and Epic Games own the cinematic VR demo showdown. Lastly, we discussed methods for profiling our own game performance to determine whether our game is being limited by the CPU or GPU, and how we can use that data to adjust and optimize our application for maximum player comfort.

In the final chapter, we will discuss the importance of game testing in the user experience design process and how to collect that data to make further design decisions. We will also learn how to finalize our game through the cooking process and prepare it for distribution. Finally, we will discuss the importance of everything we learned, how to proceed with the game prototype that we created, and look at further resources for continuing to develop VR applications.

6
Finalizing Our VR Game and Next Steps

Server 17 has come a long way from the idea we conceived at the beginning of Chapter 1, *Introducing VR Technology in Unreal Engine 4*. From our initial designs and discussions with users, we have created a game prototype with flexible systems that puts player fun and comfort first. In Chapter 5, *Creating Optimized Game Art for VR in UE4*, we discussed the limitations of game art in VR and some best practices that can be used to build the visuals that this game demands. So, where do we go from here? It's time to test!

Once we have a working prototype, it is time to test with our users and see whether some of our design ideas are right. Only the players can tell us whether we are on the right track. No design is ever perfect right out of production, and our game will often undergo several rounds of testing and redesign before we hit a version that is a winner. This is why we must test, and test often.

In this chapter, we will cover the following topics:

- The importance of game testing
- Collecting test data
- Preparing for distribution

The importance of game testing

The testing phase is an essential part of the HCD process:

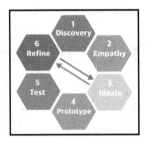

Testing is the fifth step of the HCD process

In this phase, the goal is to gain real and meaningful feedback from our players with the hopes of going over our design and improving it based on this feedback. This phase is the most important part of the process, since there is no way of knowing whether our game is fun without getting it in the hands of the players. This is also the phase where many first-time developers struggle. Many creators feel very connected to their work and view criticism of it—even constructive criticism—as criticism of them or their abilities. It is important that we separate ourselves from our work so that we can accept ideas that will improve the project. Approach all feedback with an open mind and understand that, ultimately, we get to decide which feedback we use and which we ignore. The goal is always to make the product better.

Collecting testing data

The data for testing can be collected in the following ways:

- Usability testing
- Card sort
- Expert review

There are several methods that we can use to collect feedback on our game. These methods are all designed to gather specific data from the players that can be used to improve all aspects of the game, from user interfaces to level designs. Some of them are high tech and utilize advanced methods of recording the player, such as eye movement-tracking tests. Others are very low tech and might involve having the players sort cards with certain keywords on them into categories or simply having the player try the game while you and your colleagues record the results.

Usability testing

The first method that many of us are the most familiar with is usability testing. Usability testing involves bringing testers to your location and having them test your design while you and others observe and record the results. Observing the test is similar to recording notes during an interview. Pay attention to what the user says, but also to their body language and what they do.

Here is an example: Let's say you have created a puzzle game that takes place in a labyrinth. You give ten players that fit your target demographic a chance to try the game during the alpha stage. During testing, nearly every player decides to try to jump a barrier that was placed in the level. When asked about it afterward, four players express frustration that they couldn't get over the barrier, since they thought it might be a shortcut. Nearly all thought that the barrier looked like something they should have been able to pass. How could we use this information to improve the game? One option might be to change the look of the barrier to something more impassible—maybe a wall instead of a fence. This would certainly solve the problem, but it doesn't really take advantage of what we have learned. We could build a secret reward into the area. We could adjust the barrier a bit to make it passable to a determined player and hide a reward on the other side. We could also play to the player's expectations by adding a shortcut just past the barrier if they can get past it. Finally, we always have the option to ignore this particular piece of player feedback if we felt that the change was unnecessary. Which would you choose?

Card sorting

Another method that was designed to gather player data is card sorting, which can be useful for understanding player perceptions of key features or decided what the focus of a game should be. This method comes to us from the world of psychological testing and is designed to help us understand user expectations and their understanding of your idea. Card sorting involves writing 50–60 keywords or ideas on some note cards and asking players to sort them into categories or rank them based on their importance. These could be game features such as leveling, weapon modification, or multiplayer. They could also be more abstract ideas such as what is an acceptable game time or how important is player comfort to the experience.

There are two types of card-sorting activities. Open-card sorting asks the player to organize the cards into categories and then name those categories in a way that accurately describes what is in them, while closed-card sorting is a method where players sort the cards into predefined categories to show you their knowledge of the content. Both methods have their benefits. The first allows you to test how players perceive your ideas. The second allows you to label the ideas and test your labeling, with real users.

Expert review

The final method I would like to discuss is expert review. This involves sending your game to an expert and gathering their opinions. In games, this may mean having several different experts try your product and give you feedback on specific features. This would include having a level designer test your game and give you feedback on the levels, or a UX designer giving you feedback on your interfaces and interaction systems. This method allows you to gain professional insight into areas where your team's design expertise might be weak, as often members of small teams wear multiple hats and are asked to take on tasks they know little about. However, it is important to note that this is not a substitute for having players test our game, since player feedback is always the most important type of insight we can get.

Preparing for distribution

So, we have gathered player data, reworked the design, and tested again. We might have been through this part of the design cycle several times already, but now our game is perfect and ready for release to the masses. So, it is time to cook and package a release version of the application. This process has several steps:

1. Adjust our **Project Settings.**
2. Launch the **ProjectLauncher.**
3. Set up a **Custom Launch Profile.**
4. Test the game build.

Our journey to release starts by adjusting some **Packaging** settings in our **Project Settings**:

Project Settings, showing the Blueprint Nativization option

Let's turn on **Blueprint Nativization**. This option converts our existing blueprints into C++ code, which will give us a bump in performance:

1. Find the **Blueprint Nativization** option in the **Packaging** section of the **Project Settings** menu.
2. Click the dropdown menu and choose the **Inclusive** option.

Next, choose the **Windows** option in the **Platforms** section of the menu along the left-hand side. Here, you can use your custom splash screen or a custom icon for your game. This is definitely something we should do before our game is released.

Now, we need to head over to the **ProjectLauncher**:

The Project Launcher window

From here, we can choose one of the default profiles for our launch preferences or we can create our own. Though the **WindowsNoEditor** option will likely work for us, let's try creating our own custom profile down at the bottom:

1. Toward the bottom of the launcher, click the + button to create a custom launch profile.
2. At the top of the window, double-click on the **New Profile 0** name and name this profile VRQuickStart.
3. Double-click on the words **Enter a description here** and provide a description for this profile.
4. In the project section, we can specify that we would like to use this profile for a specific project. Leave this on the default option for now.
5. Head to the **Cook** section and use the dropdown menu to choose the **By the book** option. Cooking our content removes any content that is not used and prepares our files for the specified platform.
6. Under **Cooked Platforms**, make sure that the checkbox for **WindowsNoEditor** is selected.
7. Under **Cooked Cultures**, make sure that any cultures you would like to localize for are selected. I have chosen **en-US**.
8. For **Cooked Maps**, choose the prototype map you created.
9. In the **Deploy** section of the menu, make sure that your computer is selected. Under **Variant**, choose the **WindowsNoEditor** option.
10. Finally, click the **Back** option to head back to the **Project Launcher**.

With our profile set up, it is finally time to launch our custom profile and allow Unreal to prepare our game for distribution! Click the **Launch** button for our custom profile and watch our game go through the process. Since there isn't much to our game beyond a prototype right now, the whole process will only take a few minutes. As we move to having a more complete game with art, multiple levels, and a greater degree of custom code, this process will take longer. Once it is complete, it is time to enjoy our demo!

Summary

Congratulations! We now have a packaged and complete game prototype! So, where do we go from here? With what we have learned throughout the chapters of this book, the future of our game seems vast and infinite. For some of you, you may want to continue with some of the themes that we have created with *Server 17*. For others, the goal might be to take the systems that we have designed and build and start a new game. Each system we programmed in Chapter 3, *Exploring Riveting Gameplay in Virtual Reality*, and Chapter 4, *User Interface and User Experience inside VR*, were designed to be generic and flexible, allowing the reader to take them in any direction that they wished. I can see the same systems that I interpreted as perfect for a hacking puzzle game reimagined for use in a shooter game, vehicle experience, or even a cartoon cooking game. Once you have settled on a design, build your gameplay and test with the players you have chosen to build for. Refine your idea, build some amazing looking art, and release it into the wild.

Ultimately, it is up to you to decide what becomes of this prototype. Yet, whatever you decide to do, never stop creating. We become good at what we spend our time doing. If you want to expand your skills in game design, never stop making games.

Other Books You May Enjoy

If you enjoyed this book, you may be interested in these other books by Packt:

Mastering Game Development with Unreal Engine 4 - Second Edition
Matt Edmonds

ISBN: 9781788991445

- The fundamentals of a combat-based game that will let you build and work all other systems from the core gameplay: the input, inventory, A.I. enemies, U.I., and audio
- Manage performance tools and branching shaders based on platform capabilities in the Material Editor
- Explore scene or level transitions and management strategies
- Improve visuals using UE4 systems such as Volumetric Lightmaps, Precomputed Lighting, and Cutscenes
- Implement audio-to-animation timelines and trigger them from visual FX
- Integrate Augmented Reality into a game with UE4's brand new ARKit and ARCore support
- Perform almost any game logic needed via Blueprint Visual Scripting, and know when to implement it in Blueprint as opposed to C++

Learning C++ by Building Games with Unreal Engine 4 - Second Edition
Sharan Volin

ISBN: 9781788476249

- Learn the basics of C++ and also basic UE4 editing
- Learn your way around the UE4 editor and the basics of using C++ and Blueprints within the engine
- Learn how to use basic C++ containers and data structures to store your game data
- Create players, NPCs, and monsters
- Give information to users using the UE4 UMG UI system
- Gain a basic understanding of how to use procedural programming to give your game more replay value
- Learn how UE4 can help you build projects using the hottest new technologies, such as VR and AR

Leave a review - let other readers know what you think

Please share your thoughts on this book with others by leaving a review on the site that you bought it from. If you purchased the book from Amazon, please leave us an honest review on this book's Amazon page. This is vital so that other potential readers can see and use your unbiased opinion to make purchasing decisions, we can understand what our customers think about our products, and our authors can see your feedback on the title that they have worked with Packt to create. It will only take a few minutes of your time, but is valuable to other potential customers, our authors, and Packt. Thank you!

Index